THE PROMISE

The true life story of one boy's
escape from the Baltimore ghetto.

By Alphonso Mayo

and Brian Nelson

THE PROMISE

The true life story of one boy's
escape from the Baltimore ghetto.

By Alphonso Mayo
and Brian Nelson

The Promise

ISBN: 979-8-9886465-5-6 Softbound

ISBN: 979-8-9886465-6-3 EBook

ISBN: 979-8-9886465-7-0 Hardbound

Copyright © 2023 by Alphonso Mayo

Request for information should be addressed to:

Curry Brothers Marketing and Publishing Group

P.O. Box 247 Haymarket, VA 20168

Cover Design: Robert Wesley

Executive Editing: Chantal Johnson

CURRY BROTHERS
PUBLISHING

Endorsements

- "Never underestimate the power of purpose! Alphonso Mayo's story is unbelievably transformative to those who know him, and to those who are willing to take the journey of The Promise. This book will not only inspire you but will make you question YOUR OWN PURPOSE (in the best of ways). Opening this book will open your soul to empathy, resolve, gratefulness, and humility - don't miss it! And for those of you who've never met the author, remember, life is always better with a little bit of Mayo (Alphonso Mayo, that is)."

  -Master Rick Rando (RandoSpeaks.com)

- The Promise is the real life of a man with much to share with us. Mayo's childhood experiences and life lessons are worth exploring. I was moved by the intensity of his story while being reminded of the purpose and promise of us all, regardless of one's zip code, race and/ or ethnicity, or income level. It was truly encouraging to see Mayo's intriguing life story unfold and to get excited about how his purpose was realized. Well worth the read, and this should be required reading by young and old.

  -Franklyn Baker, President and Chief Executive Officer
  United Way Of Central Way of Maryland

- I've found the book beneficial for young people who've gone through tough times. It's been helpful because sometimes teens tend to use the tough stuff we've been through as an excuse for things rather than moving past it. What struck me is how the book portrays many challenging moments but highlights what happens when you keep pushing through and not giving up. That message could resonate with youth today. The book is inspiring, although it's not the kind that would make a teen go all out and give their absolute best every day. It's motivational, but maybe not in that "take on the world" way. It could connect with some things young people deal with, but not all across the board. Yeah, I mean, many teens these days are caught up in gangs or just doing things they shouldn't be, and some of us don't even have both our parents around. In those situations, the book could hit home. For me, reading the book stirred up some strong emotions. The author's bravery and all the events they went through really got to me. It was a rollercoaster of feelings. The book lays out some intelligent approaches to helping out young people. It says something important – you can't just assume they're doing okay based on how they look, how well they do in school, or even what they say. It's about being there for them, making them feel supported, having faith in them, and showing them love. That's the natural way to have their back and help them grow. The book narrative offers insights into overcoming challenges and underscores the pivotal role of nurturing and guidance in their journey toward healing and growth.

-Jermaine Horsey, Student: Mentoring Mentors Inc.

- The Promise is a book of power, perseverance, and growth. The journey of a boy of the world, into a Man of God. A truly inspiring book that leads the reader towards discovering their potential and fostering a connection with their faith. It's not a story about one person but a story of the future of many.

-Naaman Brown, Professional Photographer
(https://www.naamanbrown.com/)

- The Promise is a must-read for anyone seeking a recipe for resiliency and fortitude in the face of seemingly insurmountable odds. With courageous vulnerability and vivid storytelling, Baltimore native son Alphonso Mayo shares his compelling memoir of survival, struggle, faith, and redemption. With deep respect and admiration I've witnessed how Alphonso serves as a hometown hero for the next generation of Baltimore's young hearts and minds. The Promise reveals the riveting backstory of what he's had to overcome to become a bright light in an often dark world for young people trying to find their way.

  -Shawn Dove, Co-Author, I Too Am America: On Loving and Leading Black Men & Boys
  (https://dovesoars.com/)

- Mayo's story, The Promise, was the most moving manuscript I have ever read. His level of transparency and vulnerability while sharing his life experiences growing up in Baltimore City was so profound. The details he provides regarding the life challenges he endured from infancy to when he finally surmounted his one true goal and ultimately keeping his promise to his beloved grandmother by finishing college, was heartfelt. As you read Mayo's words, his detailed description of his day-to-day struggles allows you to feel as if you are walking side by side with him all while trying to navigate this hustle called life. Mayo's, The Promise is by far one of my favorite books to read, and I highly recommend anyone feeling lost or alone take some time to read his life story.

  -Chantel Johnson Book Editor

- My dear brother, Mayo, has a story to tell. And believe me, you will be better off after reading it, reflecting on it, and ultimately seeing just a bit of yourself in it; I know I did. What Mayo has done so beautifully through his story is remind us that the only way we'll all collectively heal & progress is to see ourselves in each other's stories. This is doubly the case with our young people, whom Mayo has dedicated his life to loving and supporting. Let's keep telling our stories, as Mayo has led the way. Salute!

  -Sadiq Ali
  (https://millionaire-manners.com/meet-our-team/)

- Alphonso Mayo gives you a rare glimpse into what real heroes are made of by sharing his life story. This project will make you laugh, cry, and shout to the heavens with extreme frustrations because normal life is not supposed to be this hard. Mayo has created a model life for young and old to emulate, so take notice! He has endured the toughest of times, and championed on without hesitation because he had no other choice. His life proves God has a plan for all of us, and no matter how dire your life is, His Promise will sustain you.

  -Dr. Gerald D. Curry, Government Executive, Author, Professor, Life Coach, Entrepreneur

Table of Contents

Overview

The Promise is an incredible true story of Alphonso Mayo, a young African American man born at the height of the crack epidemic in 1987 to a drug addict mother who abandoned him in a drug house when he was six months old. Rescued by his Aunt and Uncle, Alphonso spent the rest of his childhood in a home filled with drugs and violence. He saw his first murder at age five and lost his first friend to gun violence—a six-year-old girl—a year later. Within his home, he endured physical abuse and hunger almost daily. He watched many family members waste away from drugs and alcohol.

When his father was released from prison, the relationship was brutal, filled with relentless physical, emotional, and psychological abuse. Surrounded by violence in school, home, and on the streets—Alphonso became violent, too. By the time he was thirteen, he had been suspended from school over 100 times, almost exclusively for fighting. Unfortunately, Alphonso's education suffered, and by the time he reached high school, he did not know how to read. His path in life seemed set. He would become a violent criminal, like members of his family.

Yet despite his crippling setbacks, The Promise is a result of determination, discipline, and resilience, all while beating the odds. Despite facing overwhelming odds, Alphonso found guidance from an unexpected ensemble of teachers. These included a drug kingpin who forbade him from dealing, a compassionate and big-hearted football coach, a devoted grandmother, and a vigilante cop who played an unconventional role in shaping Alphonso's destiny. Together, these unconventional teachers became instrumental in transforming his life for the better. At fourteen, he began the painstaking process of learning to read and controlling his violent impulses. He eventually finished high school, then college, and was able to come to terms with his past. Presently, Alphonso dedicates himself to guiding young individuals away from the hardships and challenges he encountered during his life. As the Founder and CEO of Mentoring Mentors Inc., his mission revolves around assisting youth who have experienced similar adversities, helping them recognize and unlock their full potential. The organization's mission is to develop the next generation of community leaders. His perspective on life in Baltimore provides invaluable lessons for anyone trying to understand America's troubled race relations, inner-city poverty, the war on drugs, and our broken police culture.

Finally, The Promise is a fantastic portrait of one of America's poorest black communities and our failure as a nation to provide adequate care for children at risk. With the assistance and encouragement of Brian Nelson, Alphonso started writing his memoir. Brian Nelson is the author of The Silence and the Scorpion: The Coup against Chávez and The Making of Modern Venezuela, which was named one of the best books of 2009 by

Amongst the book's highlights:

The Economist.

- **A powerful father-son story:** Alphonso was six years old when he realized that a man who sometimes stayed at his house was, in fact, his father. One day Alphonso was physically disciplined for consuming a packet of cookies. He discovered that the man inflicting the punishment was his biological father. It was the beginning of a long, painful, abusive relationship. His father's addiction to crack, coupled with intense rage, resulted in him being in constant trouble with the law. He also abused Alphonso relentlessly, usually for no reason. At age ten, Alphonso began to stand up for himself, fighting his father back. Remarkably, he started to win. By the time he reached thirteen, Alphonso found himself in an unusual role reversal, monitoring his father's actions and trying to ensure he contributed to the family's finances instead of spending it on drugs. Although his father never conquered his addiction, they were able to mend their troubled relationship.

- **An Unusual Twist on Police Vigilantism:** Alphonso's experiences with the Baltimore Police has run a gambit. He has experienced harassment, intimidation, unwarranted searches, and blatant racism. In a scenario similar to other black men killed by police, Alphonso was almost killed by a group of officers who mistook him for a murderer. Remarkably, Alphonso credits his growth and second chance in life to a vigilante cop who caught him red-handed in a case of attempted murder. Ultimately, deciding to let him go. Alphonso considered it a pivotal moment in his life and the moment he knew he had to change his ways.

- The Robin Hood of Drug Kingpins: By the time Alphonso graduated from college, most of his childhood friends were dead or in prison for drug-related crimes. Alphonso narrowly escaped the same path, primarily because of the provision and encouragement he received from the biggest drug kingpin in his neighborhood by the name of L.A. A man who paid people's rent, funded neighborhood cookouts, and didn't let his dealers sell in the hours after school. L.A. loved to watch Alphonso play football, and he knew that if this young man could stay out of the streets and the drug game, he might make the pros. One afternoon, he introduced Alphonso to all his dealers and told them, "If any of you ever let Al use or sell drugs, I'll kill both of you."

- The Real Baltimore. Alphonso grew up on North Avenue on Baltimore's west side, just two blocks from where police picked up Freddie Gray on April 12, 2015. It is an area of chronic unemployment, rampant crime, drug violence, and heavy-handed police. According to David Simon, it's "as brutal and unforgiving ghetto that America ever managed to create." This is a world that White America is just coming to understand through the viral videos of murdered black men like Eric Garner, Alton Sterling, and Freddie Gray. The Promise will bring this world to life and put a human face on inner-city America.

Gratitude Reflection

This book will feature reflections of gratitude scattered throughout its pages. These reflections are not presented in any particular order. None of the individuals who believed in me are more important than the next. Each person comes with their individual season and lessons. Some seasons are better than others, but it does not take away from the lessons I have learned.

Let me begin by thanking my father, Alphonso Mayo Sr. As a child, he never mentioned that he loved me. Innately, I knew that he did. However, I also knew that his love was limited because of his addiction. In this book, you'll get a glimpse into my father's life, which was a constant battle with abuse and addiction.

However, I would like to thank him for helping me become the man I am today. My father had the most untapped potential of the thousands of people I've met throughout my lifetime. That potential lives in me. It has become the fuel for my purpose. Thanks to my father, I am resilient and strive to be the best dad possible. I strive to give my children as much love as I can. This includes children who are not biologically mine. If not for my father's inability to be that kind of father, I'm not sure what kind of father I would be. At a very young age, I promised myself that I wouldn't be anything like my father. I've discovered that just as you can gain valuable insights from positive experiences, you can also learn from negative ones. It's about extracting the positive aspects of someone's life journey, even when faced with challenging circumstances. Thank you, Big Al; I love you more than you will ever know. You're my father, and I am proud to be your namesake. I'm not ashamed of you, and I will continue to be the best I can be by carrying on your name legacy and living up to my fullest potential.

Thank you to all the teachers who saw my potential when I could not see it in myself. Many of you believed I had the innate ability to speak, encourage, and empower others. Without you, I might have never found the courage and strength to use my voice. It is written, "Life and death are in the power of the tongue" Proverbs 18:21.

Beautifully Broken Family

For my family, the purpose of this story is not to embarrass anyone but to inspire everyone. I love you all.

- To my cousin India Mayo, thanks for all you have done for me. Although my mother was absent, you filled that void as best as you could, and your love has transformed me into the man I am today. You are more than a cousin. You are a mother, sister, cousin, and best friend. I never ask you for gifts because the love you have given me over the years alone makes me feel like the luckiest man in the world. Before I leave this world, I will do my best to make you proud.

- To my little cousins, I always strived to exemplify what was possible for us. At times, I feel like I failed you. I'm grateful that you saw something in me and embraced me like a big brother. Before the concept of Mentoring Mentors became a reality, I endeavored to pioneer it within our family, aiming to disrupt generational cycles. As the slightly older cousin, I willingly absorbed life's blows, hoping to shield you from unnecessary struggles. I've always aimed to learn and lead, providing an example to emulate. I strived to make choices aligned with what's right, demonstrating that we could forge a path different from past mistakes of our family. At times, it might have seemed like I was pushing or even bullying you, not to inflict harm but to instill a healthy fear that would guide you towards the right path. If my actions caused you pain, please understand it was never intentional and I ask for your forgiveness. I was doing my best to express love while simultaneously building a foundation for myself. My intentions were rooted in a genuine desire for your well-being and the betterment of our family's future.

- To my sister Aisha Bey, you knew me before I knew you. You called me by name. I was about ten years old and walking down Franklin town, and you looked at me and yelled, *"Lil Al."* I had no clue who you were. I took that information back to my father, who told me you were my sister. Years passed without contact, but I never forgot you. I longed for you. Ten years later, thank you for being courageous enough to walk up to me and say, *"I'm your sister."* You've been nothing but a bonus. I love you, and I will always love you.

The unknown 1st and 2nd graders

- I want to thank those first and second-graders who allowed me to tutor them during my ninth-grade year. I could not read, and they did not know that. Regardless, they considered me a big brother. Thank you for teaching me the language of reading. I don't know your names, but you saved my life and helped me achieve goals I didn't know were obtainable. I am incredibly grateful and honored that God blessed me with an opportunity to learn from you.

I was very fortunate to receive encouragement from various coaches, teachers, extended family members, and community members along my journey. Many of these informal mentors taught me the importance of always having someone in your corner. They taught me that there was nothing I couldn't do and that education was essential to my success. In addition, I learned the importance of chasing my dreams and how keeping

God's Promise would sustain me.

Lastly, thank you to all the readers. I pray you will be inspired and moved to keep going and fighting for your Promise.

"In life, we must leave things behind that we care about to grow. It may seem strange that growth comes with loss, but all losses are worth God's victories for you." -Mayo (2013)-

Dedication

This book is dedicated to God, my grandparents, my children, and a few of my brothers.

- George and Gloria Mayo
- A'mia Mayo
- A'maya Mayo
- Dylan Mayo
- Mason Mayo
- My Future Children
- Mentoring Mentors Youth

Brother's who are not here to celebrate:

- Bryan Conyers
- David Mitchell
- Emmanuel Paul
- Travis Douglass
- Travis Spencer
- Mathieu (Mears) Ali

Introduction

Once you are exposed to something "good or bad," you cannot be unexposed. It's with you forever. -Mayo-

Thank you God, for this opportunity to tell my life story. It has been a decade-long journey and one of the most challenging processes I have endured. Through it all, God, you were with me. There were moments when I felt inspired to write, but more often, I felt discouraged and ashamed. I was constantly reminded of my favorite bible verse, "My grace is sufficient for you, for my power is made perfect in your weakness. Therefore, I will boast all the more gladly of my weaknesses so that the power of Christ may rest upon me." -2 Corinthians 12:9.

God, you have allowed me to share parts of my story with others who felt inspired but did not know that I felt gravely defeated. It had to be only you allowing me to inspire others while I was going through my own private hell. Thank you for the strength to persevere. This is our story, and whosoever reads it will know that without you, there is nothing. I pray that your love, grace, and strength shine through each chapter like a ray of light.

I am sincerely grateful to share my life story, hoping it will inspire courage, faith, fortitude, and the desire never to give up. I pray this book allows others to go beyond their current circumstances and pursue their dreams. Thank you to the person opposite who decided to read my story. My life has been about overcoming challenges, adversity, and consistently redefining my resilience. I'm sure we have that in common. Despite everything I endured, I know what can be achieved if you believe in yourself. As you read about my experiences, you will learn that this is coupled with the gratification of creating something positive out of the pain. As difficult as these experiences may appear to others, they have prepared me for who I am and the work I do today.

Above all, I am not a victim. I am not proud of my humble beginnings, but I'm honored to have made it this far. If it is not apparent by now, I believe in a higher power and that our lives are like stories written by an author who infuses our end in our beginning. Secondly, I've come to understand that nothing bad occurred in my life; instead, everything I perceived as unfavorable has unfolded for a purpose. Everything I have experienced helped develop my foundation of learning, allowing me to share my story to inspire others today. Do not, I repeat, do not feel sorry for me.

It is written, "Everything happens for the good of God" Romains 8:28. If you believe nothing, I would encourage you to believe that verse. This story is about my family, our failures, resilience, and the Promise God placed on my life as a gift to my grandmother. Read as if you are in the moment with me. I want you to be present. As my big brother Dr. Eric Thomas would say, "Give it 150% of your focus." Some of the audience may need help understanding due to your race, culture, upbringing, education, environmental norms, family dynamic, and life experience. Let's push all that aside. For those from educational, professional, and health institutions, this story has nothing to do with trauma, oppression, systemic racism, or suffering. This story, however, focuses on perseverance and adversity in the face of trauma and pain.

If you begin to experience negative and sad feelings as you read, it's okay. You may empathize, but please do not feel sorry for me or any other persons I share with you. I encourage you to cry and read the book in its entirety.

Every relationship in our life has a purpose. Some are lessons, while others are blessings. Some relationships are for a lifetime, and others are temporary. No matter what the reason may be, God put that person in your life for a reason. It's up to you to discover why.

Tyler Perry, acting as "Madea," said it like this:

"Some people are like leaves on a tree. If the wind blows, they're over here and over there; they're unstable. When the seasons change, they wither and die; they're gone. But that's alright, that's some people. Most people in the world are like that. They're just there to take from the tree; they aren't there to do nothing but take and give shade now and then. That's all they can do. But don't get mad at people like that; that's who they are. They will never be anything more than A LEAF. Some people are like a branch of that tree. You must also be careful with the branches because they'll fool you. They'll make you think they're a good friend and really strong. But the minute you step out there on them, they'll break and leave you high and dry. But if you find two or three people in your life like the roots at the bottom of that tree, you are blessed because they're the kind of people who ain't going nowhere. They aren't worried about being seen, don't nobody have to know that they know you, they don't have to know what they're doing for you. But if those roots weren't there, that tree couldn't live."

You have a story:

In 2011, during my freshman year, I met Brian Nelson a.k.a Professor B, an English professor of creative writing. His class intrigued me. It was one of the few classes where I could write freely about my thoughts, fears, and feelings. I created stories about my past, refugee co-workers, and my family. It was therapeutic to some degree. In 2015, almost four years had gone by since I passed his class with little to no communication. Then, out of the blue, Professor B contacted me. He had been going through some of his old papers and stumbled upon one of the papers I wrote about my Uncle George. He contacted me via a Facebook comment and asked if we could have a conversation. Although I don't remember much of our initial conversation, he encouraged me to write a story about my life. This was the strangest idea because I did not grow up reading any books, nor could I read until the 9th grade.

My thoughts were:

- **"Why would I write a book?"**

- **"Who would read it?"**

- **"Why would anyone care?"**

Little did I realize Professor B was trying to be a root. I was not much of a writer during my educational journey. I didn't understand the process of writing a book, and I always struggled with English and grammar because I did not have enough experience reading and writing during my childhood. I wrote a few songs that never came to life during high school. I wrote a poem here and there but kept it to myself. To write a book sounded utterly ridiculous. It wasn't until college that I picked up books to read for pleasure. Two of my favorite books are:

- The Other Wes Moore: One Name, Two Fates Book by Wes Moore

- Never Die Easy: The Autobiography of Walter Payton Book by Don Yaeger and Walter Payton.

Here's another disclaimer, "I didn't feel qualified to write a book of any kind."

- Children's books

- Nursery rhymes

- Sportsbooks

- High School Yearbooks

I was very uncomfortable sharing my past. I didn't want anyone to know most of what I'd experienced growing up and later shared with Mr. B. Hell; I tried my best to forget it and often pretended that it didn't even exist. However, with his inspiration, support, and encouragement, I felt I had someone there to support, listen, and guide me through the process. I had someone that I could trust. I later reached out and agreed that if he helped me, I would write my story. During the initial years of conversation with Professor B, I constantly doubted that the book would be completed unless he wrote it himself. I lacked confidence in my own writing abilities.

In 2016, I took my son to the Kennedy Krieger Institution for an intellectual evaluation to determine if he had autism. The office we visited felt strangely familiar, although my memory of it was foggy. It felt like I had been there before. Curious, I asked the receptionist about any previous evaluations I might have had as a child. To my surprise, she confirmed that I had indeed undergone an educational evaluation there.

After following the proper procedures to retrieve the evaluation, I discovered that there were many things I was not supposed to do independently. When I learned they wanted to put me in a special educational class where they discouraged reading books on my own, it really hit me hard. Which is why I decided to write my own story, regardless of the time or effort required. No matter how difficult it got or what obstacles I had to overcome.

Writing has always been difficult for me. Writing this book has been a severely complex process for me. Due to my athletic abilities, specific attributes that coincided with my learning diagnosis were always overlooked. Throughout school, when the teacher would call on me to read, my heart would quiver, resulting in me experiencing extreme levels of anxiety and anger. Bibliophobia took over, and I couldn't read the words on the pages.

DIAGNOSES:

1. Learning disabilities in reading and written language

RECOMMENDATIONS:

1. A meeting should be held at Al's school to review the results of this evaluation and to arrange special education services to address his significant learning disabilities in reading and written language. Al will need intensive individualized efforts to help him develop his basic reading and writing skills. He appears to have marked difficulty with

17692   03/20/2001

707 North Broadway   Baltimore, Maryland 21205   (410)502-9000/Telephone   (410)502-9034/Fax   (410)502-9806/TTY

ALPHONSO MAYO
00082633
Page 7 of 7

Mayo, Alphonso
MRN 08-26-33

---

phonological processing, and his problems with visual organization may also contribute to reading problems. All of his teachers will need to be aware of his very limited reading and writing skills and adapt instruction to him appropriately. Al cannot be expected to read textbooks and should be provided with any textbooks used on audiotape. His school can obtain audiotape textbooks through the Readings for the Blind or Dyslexic program, which can be contacted at 800-221-4792. Al also will not be able to write down class notes, assignments, or other important information, and should have any essential written material provided for him. Assessment of his learning will need to be done orally until his basic reading and writing skills improve markedly. Careful consideration will be needed for planning an appropriate high school curriculum. Vocational as well as purely academic goals may be appropriate.

I would experience various levels of rage, resulting in me lashing out at my teachers. This was my coping mechanism to mask my embarrassment, now I am being asked to write a book.

One conversation after another, Mr. B and I met for 14-plus months until his family moved. We would get together every week, and I would share stories about growing up on Baltimore's West Side, a very tough and impoverished area of the city. Over the years, I would start and stop the writing process to reflect and, at the same time, stop out of fear. I wrote most of these chapters with tears in my eyes, crying out to God, inspired because I knew someone would benefit from my story after reading this. I want this story to be one of those, **"If he did it, so can I."** Better yet, **"If he did it, I will do it too!"** Well, I did it. And now, you're holding the book in your hand and I am incredibly proud.

"Your beginning is just that, your beginning. It's not the end. It's not your end." -Mayo-

CHAPTER 1

BIGGEST MISTAKE AND MISTAKEN IDENTITY:
Then came the night that I almost killed my
father and the time I was nearly killed

My life almost ended in a case of mistaken identity, like those that are all too common in America's inner cities. But three things happened that kept me alive. First, I was so surprised that I didn't run. Which quite honestly was my first reaction to seeing cops. Second, Travis' mother came running out of her house screaming, "He's just a kid!" That made them hesitate. And finally, the fact that there were eight officers, and not two or one, I believe, checked their impulses.

Whenever I hear a helicopter, I think about it, black hooping shorts with a white stripe, black sneakers, and a white tee shirt.

One day after school, I went looking for my friends Bryan and Travis. This became my routine. I knocked on Bryan's door first and got no answer. So, I walked over to Travis's house just an eye distance away. Travis' mom boyfriend, Carlos, answered. He's a huge guy that looked like he has done a lot of hard time in prison and spent the majority of it lifting weights.

Carlos: **"Travis isn't at home, Mayo."**

Around this time, I heard the familiar sound of a helicopter, a common occurrence in my neighborhood. Not thinking much of it, I started walking back home. I wasn't paying much attention to the increasingly louder chopper flying nearby. Although the noise grew, I dismissed it, thinking they were likely searching for someone in the woods behind Bryan's house. Lost in thought with my head down, pondering, **"Where could Bryan and Travis be?"** I suddenly looked up and was startled to see three police officers with their guns drawn sprinting towards me. I turned and looked back to see five more police coming out of the woods towards me. All yelling,

"Get on the ground!"

"GET ON THE GROUND NOW!"

I thought, **"Who are they talking to?"**

18

"Get on the fucking ground!"

Then I realized they were talking to me.

I remembered thinking to say, **"Why?"** But right before the word was out of my mouth, an officer knocked me down from behind and had me on the ground, pushing my head down against the pavement with his hand on the back of my neck and a gun in my face. All the officers surrounded me with their guns drawn. They were hyped up and angry, threatening to kill me. By now, the neighbors noticed, and Carlos and Travis's mom were running towards me.

"What are you doing?" she yelled.

"He's only a kid! He just got out of school."

They began searching me thoroughly, checking my pockets and my waistband. Travis's mom continued yelling.

"He's just a kid! He's just a kid!"

With my face pressed against the pavement, I finally heard one of the cops speaking into his radio, "It's not him. We got the wrong guy."

They were looking for an African-American male in a white shirt, black shorts with a white stripe, and black tennis shoes who killed someone on Hillsdale Avenue a few blocks away from Bryan's house.

Cops: **"Get up, go in the house, and don't let me see you back out here."**

As I pushed myself off the pavement, all I could think about was staring down the barrel of the officer's gun. I had only seen stuff like that in movies and never thought that would happen to me. I couldn't understand why the officers were so agitated and hostile, menacingly threatening to take my life. It wasn't long after that when I had another run-in with the Baltimore Police that changed my perspective forever.

Everyone was asleep when my father came to the back of the house in the middle of the night. He was high out of his mind and wanted to come inside. He dared not go to the front door because he knew my Grandfather was sleeping in the living room and would never let him in. So he came to the back door, underneath my Grandma's bedroom window. He started calling up.

"Let me in the fucking house."

But Mama could tell he was high and belligerent and that letting him in would cause more trouble. It always did. When he realized she wasn't giving in, he flipped out.

"Open the fucking door! Open this door, you fucking bitch!"

"I'll kill all of you."

"I don't care."

Since childhood, Mama and I shared the same bed, a longstanding custom that forged a bond between us. I layed in bed listening to him. I knew Mama and the whole neighborhood could hear him. It's four in the morning, and his yelling persists for an hour, stretching into two. I listened, discouraged, as he kept repeating these ugly things over and over.

"Open the fucking door! You whore."

"My son is going to die. He's sick."

As I listened, I became mad, which turned into anger. I was so tired of the embarrassment and abuse my family suffered because of him.

"Say one more thing about my grandma," I thought. **"Just one more thing."**

He yells.

"Open the door, you fucking bitch."

I slipped on my black hooping shorts with the white stripe and went downstairs. It had been awhile since my dad and I fought. The floor was cold as I walked to our pantry, where we kept our canned goods and hardware supplies. I grabbed an antique wooden shovel and opened the door. There he stood. After standing outside in the middle of the night the temperatures dropped to frigid levels, he appeared with a still look on his face. Shivering uncontrollably. His body seemed frozen, each movement a struggle against the biting cold. Once he saw me, he rushed me. **"Come on, bitch,"** he said. He was so high. He was moving slowly and uncoordinated. He made for an easy target. I swung the shovel with all my might, connecting with the flat part against the side of his head. I heard a loud thud. He fell to the ground, holding his head. Unconsciously I kept swinging the shovel.

BANG!

BANG!

BANG!

BANG!

I was so enraged. I kept swinging until the shovel broke. He was no longer making sounds or moving. My grandmother rushed to see what happened. I could barely make out what she was saying but I heard her utter, **"Call the ambulance."** Blood was pouring out from his head and ears. The Police and Paramedics arrived at the same time. When the paramedics saw the body, they stopped. He looked bad lying there, not moving, and with all the blood, they must have thought he was dead. Slowly, the paramedics turned my father and checked for a pulse. They couldn't find one.

The cops started questioning me. I was so angry, I told the truth.

"...All he does is hurt us."

"He just kept calling Mama out of her name."

I could tell the first cop was new. Growing up in Baltimore, you pick up on things like that. He was doing everything by the book. When I finished my story he said,

"You're under arrest. Put your hands behind your back."

At that moment, I knew I was going away for a long time. Even though I was a minor this was murder and if I was lucky, attempted murder. They would send me to Charles H. Hickey, Jr School. It's called a school, but it's not. It is an all-male detention center ran by the Maryland Department of Juvenile Services. It's a prison for youth. They can keep you there until you're 18.

Unregretful, I put my hands behind my back. Then the other cop who was big and stocky with biker tattoos, put his hand on the rookie's shoulder.

"Hold on a minute," he said, **"We didn't actually see what happened here?"**

That's when I realized the older cop knew my dad. He turned to me.

"When you came outside, you found him like this, right?"

Me: **"What?"**

"When you came outside, you found him like this, right?"

I nodded in agreement. He picked up the pieces of the broken shovel and gave them to the rookie.

"Here, make these disappear."

The rookie stared at him momentarily, processing the request, then gave a breathy laugh, doing as he was told. When he was out of earshot, the older cop turned to me.

"Look, go to school, get out of this, save yourself."

Then he put a ten-dollar bill in my fist. They took my father in the ambulance. By the time the police filled out their reports, it was time for school. The older cop called for the paddy wagon to give me a ride. Ironically, the officer driving the paddy wagon that morning was one of the coaches for the youth football team I played for. The Northwest Bulldogs. He knew me as a strong player, but I was broken in that moment. When we got to the school, the coach-officer looked at me and said,

"You're going to be okay."

Then he reached into his pockets and gave me five dollars. When I got home from school, no one said anything to me, and I kept my mouth shut. It was like that for days. It was over a week before we found out my dad would survive. He suffered a significant traumatic brain injury. For years after that, he was plagued with migraines. He also has permanent memory loss. He is often convinced that things happened at certain times, but he's years off. He had no memory of what happened that night. He doesn't know I am responsible. Well, until he reads this. That moment changed my life. When the rookie cop said,

"Put your hands behind your back."

I was sure that was the end for me. Any dreams I had were gone—I would be locked up until I was eighteen, at least. But I'd been given a second chance. I knew I had to break the cycle. Until then, I had been doing the same thing repeatedly. I was entangled in fights almost every other day at school. It became my unfortunate norm—engage in a fight, face suspension, return briefly, get into another altercation, and repeat the suspension cycle.

I had now been suspended way too many times to count. Anytime I was faced with a challenge, my response was to fight. I was becoming a product of my surroundings, home, and community. Ultimately another violent Black boy.

I knew I needed to change; I just didn't know how. It was my first year in high school, which was an opportunity to recreate myself. However, I was not sure how to accomplish this. Worse, I had no one in my family to provide any direction.

Reflecting on the incident of being mistaken for an adult, I now understand the unfair treatment that Black boys often face. Growing up in poverty and facing the challenges that many of our communities face forces Black boys to mature quickly. In the eyes of society, the justice system, and some police officers, black boys are not seen as kids. There is no empathy for us. If I had reacted differently or resisted in any way, I would probably be dead, and this story wouldn't be possible. In one scenario, I was almost killed in a case of mistaken identity. In the other, a cop showed empathy because he understood exactly where my arrest could have led to. A life marked by anger, violence, and criminality, echoing the path of my father—a narrative too often followed by many young boys in inner-city neighborhoods.

Recognize that each choice you have made until now has either given you a great outcome or a lesson. Both are valuable. In fact, both are necessary. – Lisa Nichols-

CHAPTER 2
BROKEN FOUNDATIONS DON'T HOLD UP

In Toure Roberts' book, "Wholeness," he explains that we all are born with cracks in our foundations. We are born with brokenness from birth, and our cracks turn to chasms over time. There are three significant factors.

- Generational Brokenness: This is the brokenness we inherit from parents, grandparents, and even many generations before them.

- Social Brokenness: We live in a broken world, which means there is brokenness in our culture at large. examples include poverty, racism, sexism.

- Personal Brokenness: This is the brokenness we experience when we are devalued or traumatized.

When You're Born, You Look Like Your Parents. When You Die, You Look Like Your Choices. -Unknown-

Let me begin by acknowledging that I have experienced all three levels of brokenness. Frankly, there are more levels than just three, and I have also experienced those. I grew up in West Baltimore. Seventeen people lived in our house, many of whom were on a first-name basis with the police. Three generations, my grandparents, George and Gloria Mayo, their sons, George, Riccas, and my dad Alphonso, Sr. their daughters, Teresa, Darlene, and Lolita. Lastly, my cousins India, Andre, Tasha, Teila, Demetrius, Solita, James, Davante and me. Between all of us, everyone slept in every room except the kitchen.

"In Baltimore, beauty and chaos live side by side." -Ron Cassie-

I was born during the crack epidemic. Both of my parents were addicts. My mother and father were addicted to crack cocaine, and their addictions consumed their lives. I don't have any birth photos, baby pictures, or any tangible or visible proof of me as a baby. There are no snapshots capturing a proud mother holding me in her arms or a father showcasing me to the world. My father had his battles but had been clean most of his life until my older sister, Ashley, died. My guess is that was his breaking point. After that, he started using crack and getting into trouble. When I was born, thirteen months later, he was in jail. My mother used drugs and other substances throughout her pregnancy. I was born with multiple complications causing two holes in my heart. When I was six months old, my mom abandoned me in the basement of a crack house. My Aunt Lita and Uncle George eventually found me. After that, I lived with my paternal grandparents in a row house on West North Avenue, an area famous for drugs and violence.

Being raised in a family that constantly struggled with addiction and mental health issues meant my childhood was filled with turmoil and instability. Constant uncertainty led to a sense of anxiety and fear in my life. But the worst part of it all was the continual absence of my mother and the abuse from my father. Throughout my childhood, my father was in and out of jail, and when he wasn't, he was constantly abusing me verbally and physically. Growing up, I never felt loved by my parents. I felt like I didn't matter. As time went on, those feelings became increasingly difficult to shake off, and they began to affect my other relationships. As a child, I did not understand why my father was always in trouble or why neither of them couldn't be there for me. All I knew was that their absence left a gaping hole in my heart that no surgery could mend.

What I've come to understand is that not all brokenness is created equally. In families like mine, you don't even get to choose your brokenness. It's not based on your own choices or actions; it's a generational curse. Before you even have a chance to learn about mental health, your mental well-being has already been affected by the decisions of the adults who were supposed to care for you.

Generational brokenness robs you of your innocence. Many of my friends and I had to grow up faster than we would have liked. It becomes a way of protecting yourself, a coping mechanism for dealing with the harshness of the struggles placed upon you by others.

I wasn't surprised that my family was well-known by the Baltimore City Police Department. When the cops would knock on our door, they'd ask, **"Who is it this time?"** and list off the usual suspects. In any given week, the police would come to our house four to five times. In fact, if I were to write out the police records of everyone I lived with, it would fill several pages ranging from first-degree assault, second-degree assault, arson, possession, prostitution, and burglary. This may be unusual to most, but this was normal for my family.

Everyone seemed to be at odds with one another. Fighting was how they solved their differences. If not fighting, belittling, and tearing one another down with harsh and brutal words. We never had table talks at dinner. We never talked about education, finances, or religion. We didn't even have family reunions. This is the only life I knew growing up—a challenging start to my journey which led to the cracks in my broken foundation. With nothing but violence surrounding me, I learned at a very young age that I had to be tough, hide my feelings, and never show weakness. In my world, you were never safe because someone would always hurt or take from you if they could, whether in the street, in school, or in your house.

In my neighborhood, it always puzzled me how so many people seemed to be living duplicate lives. Even now, I struggle to fully articulate how growing up in Baltimore and other urban cities shape social norms for many black people. Our neighbors mirrored the norms in my family—violence was expected and always on display. Positive attitudes, education, proper word phrasing, good grammar, and healthy relationships were not embraced.

As a child, you absorb these norms through observation and pick up on people's body language and nonverbal cues. You mimic what you see, and it becomes your norm. Even in friendships, there's a lack of trust. Friendships are rooted in shared trauma and trauma bonds. Even when people love you, it's hard to trust, because those who were supposed to love you first, hurt you.

Due to my childhood experiences, I was unaware of my struggles with post-traumatic stress, depression and anxiety. This lasted throughout my adolescent years. Talk about the cracks in my foundation. I was born into a crack-addicted, dysfunctional, poor, and overall broken family. My foundation was a mixture of two crack addicts' poor habits and instability. CRACKS would have been a blessing. Unfortunately, I was fractured, fragmented, and unwanted.

"Who says all foundations are built strong, but even the fractured ones can be repaired." -Mayo-

CHAPTER 3

CRACK BABY

In my search for God, I once read a scripture that says, ***"I knew you before I formed you in your mother's womb. Before you were born, I set you apart and appointed you as my prophet to the nations."*** I would often question and wonder if God knew me. I mean, really knew me! I must have read this verse countless times and never believed this scripture's relevance to my personal life.

When I was 16, I decided to visit my father during his time in a mental health ward. It was a difficult decision, but no one else in my family cared to visit. During the visit, I mustered up the courage to ask about my sister, someone I rarely heard him mention.

"Who's Ashley?"

As the words left my mouth, I could sense a shift in the air. The tension in the room became heavy, and it was as if the weight of unspoken pain and trauma had suddenly risen to the surface. My dad looked at me, his eyes filled with a mixture of surprise, sadness, and a deep, unspoken sorrow.

He began to speak, his voice strained with emotion. He told me that he thought about her every day, a fact that was never apparent in his daily demeanor. And then, in a moment of vulnerability that I had never seen before, he shared with me his last memory of her.

The pain in his voice was raw and heartbreaking. It was clear that this was a memory he carried with him every day, a memory that haunted him in ways I could never fully understand. In that moment, I realized the depth of his love for my sister and the immense pain he felt at her loss.

On July 29, 1986, my sister Ashley Nicole Mayo was born healthy and beautiful. My father was incredibly excited because it was his first child, and all he wanted to do was protect and provide for her. One day, as she slept in her crib, he watched over her and kissed her.

Al, *"Come here,"* Flumsy said. *"And bring the baby with you."*

"Okay."

As he picked her up, he said to her, *"You are so beautiful."*

"Al, lay her here."

He placed her seamlessly and perfectly between them.

"I love you, little baby," He says.

My father, a new parent, did not expect that to be his last memory of her. At two months, Ashley died. The next morning when he woke up he yells,

"She's not moving, Flumsy."

"She's not breathing, Flumsy."

"CALL SOMEONE!"

"Baby, wake up, please wake up."

On September 19th, 1986, Ashley died from crib death. I don't think either of my parents recovered from my sister's passing. My father was an inspiring artist and car mechanic, but he started selling and using drugs more heavily and getting into trouble to cope with his guilt. He lost his ambitions and became a full-blown crack addict who consistently went to jail. He took out his frustration on his family. His words always cut deep; if that didn't work, his punches would finish the job. My mother's story was different; she was a hyper-sexual teen, and Ashley was her second child. At age 16, she had a baby boy whose name was Michael, aka Little Fella. Because she was an adolescent, Little Fella's father moved him to North Carolina to care for him. She lost Little Fella to his father, and she could do little to nothing about it. After the passing of Ashley, I believe she lost her self-esteem and was shattered. I don't know, but my guess is she started using drugs heavily to cope with the trauma of losing her children.

On October 1st, 1987, at 4:49 pm, my mother gave birth to me. I was underweight, with two holes in my heart—an aspect I've always attributed to both of my parents. Additionally, I suffered from withdrawal symptoms of crack cocaine. My parents, 19-year-old Veronica Perry (Flumsy) and 31-year-old Alphonso Mayo (Big Al).

After hearing my father's story I often felt my sister Ashley got the best of my parents because when I was born, Big Al was in jail on a minor drug charge and Flumsy consumed drugs, cigarettes, and various substances during her pregnancy. Instead of the typical joyous atmosphere that accompanies the arrival of a new baby, the hospital found itself questioning whether my mother was a suitable parent.

For me, there was no welcome home celebration. No hugs and kisses, just a baby boy who became a casualty of his parents' depression and drug addiction. Throughout my childhood I felt like a casualty rather than a prophet. How could God know me when my beginnings seemed destined to contribute to Baltimore's negative statistics? What type of God would do that?

When I was six months old, it was rumored that the police raided a house on Division Street and that "Flumsy" was being arrested, and that she left the newborn in the basement of one of those houses. My Aunt got the news from one of the local drug dealers. That evening, my Uncle George and Aunt Lita ran to retrieve me before the police called Child Protective Services. My mother has a different story.

As my Aunt Lita tells it, I was crying inconsolably, with my face red and sore. It was such a cold day, and I was only wearing a diaper. She did everything she could to calm me. She wrapped me in a t-shirt because my little body was trembling, and when I finally settled down, she went to change me and found two drug vials in my diaper. Ones she would later use. After that, I lived with my paternal grandparents in a row house on West North Avenue. Three generations in a little over 900 sq ft. That's where I began sleeping with Grandma—a custom until my sophomore year of high school.

In the 80's this horrifying birth description was not unusual, especially in Black Communities, where drug and substance addiction was prevalent. This was my beginning, and if it were not for the love and graciousness of a loving grandmother, I probably would not have made it this far. I owe my life to my grandmother because she cared for me best when no one else would.

Even with all her love, my upbringing was chaotic. At first I blamed my parents for my negative childhood experiences. Then I blamed God because my parents were victims of their own unfavorable circumstances and communities. They lacked the inner skills and discipline needed to overcome the multitude of challenges and problems they faced. Some could say they were victims, and I unfortunately became a casualty of their circumstances. Which led me to being a, *"Crack Baby."*

I hated God. I blamed God for everything—I wasn't satisfied with my family, and I despised the circumstances I faced. I felt like God had set me up for failure. I questioned God's purpose for me, asking why God placed me with my family, why had God allowed my mother to give birth to me, why God allowed my family to be poor, why God allowed us to live in a dangerous neighborhood, I even questioned why God wouldn't just take my life.

Most people only have vague memories of their early childhood experience, but I'll never forget mine. Winston Churchill said it best, *"Success is not final, failure is not fatal, it is the courage to continue that count,"* **and** *"If you're going through hell, keep going."* Well I was living in hell. As a child with limited choices, I decided I did not want to be like my family. I knew I would take my chances without a blueprint or roadmap because it seemed more promising than the outcomes I witnessed growing up. They say that children exposed to crack cocaine in utero were often labeled as destined for lives of physical and mental disabilities, but somehow God protected me and called me a prophet.

"The most dangerous creation of any society is the man who has nothing to lose." -James Baldwin-

CHAPTER *4*

SHOTS IN THE NIGHT ARE NOT THE ONLY THING SCARY

One early evening, my cousins and I were sitting on the front stoop when a dealer pulled out a shotgun and killed a man no more than sixty yards from me. The stoop, consisting of five to six steps, is where we would watch the neighborhood, play, sit, watch cars go by, and hang out. I can still see it in my mind like it happened yesterday. There was a corner store in our neighborhood where you could always purchase the basic needs on any given day. This place became the hangout for young children who were always buying candy, chips, and sodas, and parents stopping in to buy the essentials to make dinner. It wasn't a market, but it was convenient. The corner store was across the street from a liquor store that seemed to stay busy. It seemed like the liquor store was where all the action was!

My cousins and I were sitting on the front stoop. I glanced slightly to my left, and in slow motion, a dealer pulled out a shotgun with the intent of killing a rival. I froze, petrified because it felt like he had aimed directly at me. **BOOM!** It went off, hitting the other dealer in the back. All the bystanders sitting on their stoops scattered in a wild panic. I could hear women screaming, but I couldn't make sense of the yelling, but I kept my eyes on the shooter. People were running towards me. Seemingly in slow motion. Then I felt a ripping pain in my shoulder as my cousin yanked me up by the arm, hurtling me into the vestibule of our house. I was too young to know what was going on, but my cousin was terrified! She kept yelling,

"Someone just got shot!"

"Someone just got shot!"

"Oh my God, he killed him!"

I had just witnessed my first murder, and then came sirens, accompanied by police with the flickering of their lights ricocheting around the walls of our house. Before that day, I would often hear gunshots in my neighborhood but never realized what they actually were. Now I knew, and I was terrified. From then on, whenever I was lying in bed at night and heard gunshots, I knew someone was being killed. In 1991, 304 people were killed. In 1992, 333 people were killed, primarily by gunfire. There was a unique ambivalence that had settled in my neighborhood. As a child, after that exposure, I just thought I would succumb to gun violence one day. Unfortunately, over time, hearing gunshots became the norm. Surprisingly, it appeared that everyone had grown indifferent to the sound of gunfire. While the shots in the night were undoubtedly unsettling, some of the most severe violence I witnessed occurred within the walls of my own home.

Our neighborhood was infamous for drugs and violence. They sold drugs on the corners, and the dealers rode dirt bikes up and down the sidewalks where we played. I can still remember the sounds they made— the chain in the gears, the sound of the rubber skidding on cement— and that sound is forever infused in my mind.

"Braaaaaap……Braaaaaap…..Braaaaaap."

I always felt out of sorts between the gun violence in the streets and the violence in the house. Nothing ever felt settled, calm, or comforting to me. As I reflect on those early days, life just seemed to be chaotic every single day.

In second grade, my friend Evie was shot in the face at Sonny's convenience store at the end of the next block. She and I had gone there dozens of times together after school, and it was only fate that I wasn't with her that day. These events brought home the lethality of my environment. It didn't matter if you were good or bad. If you were a dealer or a kid. No one was off-limits, and death could come for you anytime. Violence was pervasive—One murder after another and a constant stream of fights, I began to grasp the inherent violence within my world. However, many more lessons were awaiting me. Like I already explained on my first day of school, I got suspended for hitting a classmate in the nose, causing it to bleed. Honestly, I believed that engaging with peers through violence was the norm. Then came the first time I was beaten by a stranger. In the first grade, a third-grade girl with cornrows and light brown skin ruthlessly attacked me. There was no reason for it. She just did it for fun.

When I got home, my cousins asked me what happened. I told them. They calmed me down and assured me everything would be all right; they'd take care of it. The following day, at roll call, everyone stood out in our school's concrete courtyard. My cousins told me to point her out, so I did. They approached her and started pushing her around.

"Wait until later," my big cousin Tisha said.

As promised, after school, we banked, known as" jumped her". Four against one. I remember it was by the church near our house. My cousins shoved her back and forth for a while, then Tisha hit her in the head, and she fell to the ground. Just the day before, I was in her position.

"Little Al, hit her," My cousin Teila said. I punched her in the face. My cousins egged me on. *"That's it. Hit her again."* So I punched her over and over again. The shame and humiliation of the day before was still fresh in my mind, almost as new as the feeling of power and vindication I felt standing over this girl. Perhaps I did not think of it, but I decided that I never wanted to feel humiliated like that again and that if any kid talked bad about me or my family, I'd fight them. In hindsight, it was a terrible idea, but I felt, and maybe it was true, that I had no alternative.

To survive in this environment, I had to be violent. It wasn't a path I chose willingly, but one that seemed forced upon me. It felt like a cruel reality. In that world, you were either the predator or the prey, with no middle ground. I didn't want to be violent. I didn't want to see the fear in others' eyes, but it seemed like there was no other way to navigate my harsh reality.

Every day was a battle for survival, a constant struggle to protect myself from harm. I've shared with you before that in school, I'd fight, get suspended, go back for a few days, and then fight again, leading to another suspension. Thanks to No Child Left Behind, I never failed in class, but my life grade was likely to be an F. And the F stood for **FUCKED!**

That's what life felt like for me. I was "Fucked" even when I thought I was safe, I wasn't. Not only was I abandoned in a basement, but I was also sexually molested and lost my virginity in the basement. A couple of weeks following the incident with the girl in 3rd grade, my cousin Tisha decided to have a get-together with some of her friends.

"Little Al, come here and play operations with us!" She yelled from the basement.

Me: *"Here I come."*

"Okay, here's how we play, Little Al; grab the tweezers and remove the bones without hitting the sides."

Me: *"Okay."*

My cousin was several years older than me. I knew she wasn't an adult, but because she was much taller and stronger, there was a level of respect and authority. Whatever she said to do, I was going to do. So we played the game with her friends.

"Little Al, this is easy, and you're good. Do you want to play the game with my friends?"

Me: *"Okay."*

When I turned around, her friend, whom I had never met, legs were open.

"Little Al, you're going to put your ding-a-ling right there."

Me: *"Okay."*

"Now go back and forth."

Me: *"Okay."*

I didn't know what I was doing, but my senses told me that we could get into trouble, and I became overwhelmed and nervous, and after a few pumps, I peed inside of her.

Friend: *"Oh my God, he peed in me."*

I could hear the laughter but also the anger in her voice.

Friend: *"Get off of me."*

I moved back, and I pulled up my shorts.

"Little Al, if you say anything, I'm going to tell that you peed in her, and you're going to get in trouble."

The fear of facing repercussions from my Uncle George, and even worse, abuse from my father, prevented me from opening up. I suppose I didn't want to get into trouble. As a child, feeling confused and lost, I absorbed the message that I wasn't expected to become much of anything. Although I wasn't aware of the statistics at the time—indicating a higher likelihood of being dead or in jail by my 25th birthday—I already had a sense that my life and the lives of those around me weren't worth much in the grand scheme of life.

My innocence and inner sense were taken from me. The reality of my future rang out like the shots in the night as I was constantly reminded that this was all my life would be and there was nothing I could do about it.

Trauma does not allow children to develop in a healthy, sustainable way. It's less about growth and development and more about survival. -Mayo-

CHAPTER 5

FOR NAME SAKES

"My father had more potential than anyone I've ever met, but he indirectly taught me that potential is not the promise or the destination. He lived only in his potential, and never became much of anything."
-Mayo-

When my father was out of jail, he made my life a living hell. He was a maniac; plain and simple. A strung-out junkie with a hair-trigger temper and a bad case of LMS, Little Man Syndrome. He didn't fight much on the street because he was so small. He was a little dog with a loud bark and no bite. He wanted to dominate everyone in the house by picking fights over the most trivial things like the last piece of bread, his spot on the sofa, and the remote control. He was like a child having temper tantrums. He never cared about the consequences, and he'd say so himself.

"Call the Fucking Police."

"What the Fuck are you going to do about it?"

"I don't give a fuck. I'll knock your brains out."

His favorite saying was, *"I'll knock your brains out."* at which he loved to remind you that he wasn't afraid of being arrested again. *"I don't give a fuck about going to jail. It doesn't make any difference."*

He never spent time with me, encouraged me, or tried to teach me anything. When I was seven, I had to have heart surgery to fix the two holes in my heart. I was in the hospital for ten days. He never came once. I started playing football at age nine. By the time I graduated high school, I had played in over 200 games. My father came to one game. It wasn't simply that my father didn't care about me; he seemed to want to physically and psychologically hurt me.

My father was in jail so much that for the longest time, I didn't know he was my father. I thought my Uncle George was my father. It wasn't until the first time he whipped me that I realized who he was. When my

Grandfather gave me a dollar to go to the convenient store, I bought two packs of lemon cookies. I was so happy that I ate the first pack on the walk back. When I came through the vestibule, there sat a man.

"Come here," he said.

"What's in the bag?"

"Cookies," I said.

"What happened to the first pack?"

"I ate them on the walk back."

He took the bag of cookies, spun me around, and started beating me. The pain shot through my back into my head, and I became nauseous. All I could do was wait for someone to stop him, but no one did. I was so confused because whenever anyone tried to hurt me, my Grandma would always intervene. However, this time was different; because he was my father, she didn't intervene. That was the beginning of years of abuse by my father. In my community, it was common for parents to beat their kids for no reason, but my father would do it almost every day.

When I was nine, we moved to a better house in Cherry Hill, and I hoped things would improve. He pulled me aside one day before the holidays and asked me to make a Christmas list. Until then, he had never bought me anything—no clothes, shoes, or toys for my birthday or holidays—but with high hopes I made my list. I wanted to believe so badly that my father loved me. I still remember my list:

- Black Timberland Boots

- Video games for my Sega Genesis

- Clothes

I was so happy. Finally, he was doing something for me, and I couldn't wait. On Christmas Eve, I walked to the other end of the street where my father was staying with his girlfriend, Ms. Donna. Her son Tyrell welcomed me in. Tyrell was my age, and we were friends because we both played football. As the night went on, Tyrell and I talked, and I shared my Christmas list with him. I was so excited I couldn't sleep that night. It felt like I woke up every 15 minutes out of excitement. The following day, Tyrell woke me up and said,

"Come on! Let's go see what we got."

When I got to the Christmas tree, I searched for my presents, but they all said,

"To Tyrell, From Mommy."

"To Tyrell, From Big Al and Mommy."

As time passed, I felt terrible, but I tried to make the best of it. I turned to Tyrell,

"Can I help you open up your presents?"

Without hesitation, he tossed me a box. Inside were three video games for his Sega Genesis. My heart dropped. Then he opened his next box, a pair of Black Timberland Boots. I sat there, heartbroken, feeling utterly numb as Tyrell opened the rest of his presents. My father walked into the room and smiled at Tyrell,

"Do you like it?"

Tyrell gave him a huge smile and nodded enthusiastically. I sat looking out the window so my father couldn't see my face. Once he left the room, I picked up my coat and walked out. As I walked through the alley, I kept my head down, tears rolling down my face; The familiar pain of feeling rejected and not being loved made me feel like my heart would seize in my chest. Each breath became shorter and shorter as I gasped for air.

I should have known not to let my guard down. When I walked in the back door of my grandparents' house, my grandmother asked, ***"What's wrong?"*** But I couldn't speak. I walked by the Christmas tree, with all the presents with my name on them, and went upstairs to the room me and my grandma shared. That pain turned into more anger and hatred for my father.

Every little boy's first superhero is their father; when his hero never shows up to rescue him, he become villains. -Mayo-

It wasn't just that my father was a bad father; my life seemed to be on repeat. Every day in my house was the same—the ghetto abusive version of Groundhog Day, and I had no way of escaping it. By the early afternoon, Uncle Riccas would be drunk. Then my dad would come by the house, strung out and belligerent, looking for a fight. He'd start picking on Uncle Riccas, who was an easy target because he was wasted, and before long, they'd come to blows. On other days, Uncle Riccas and my father would start fights with my granddad, another easy target because he was blind. My guess is whoever was an easy target would be next. Some days I tried to calm my dad down before it escalated, but that usually meant he'd turn on me.

"Who the fuck are you talking to?"

He'd say, unbuckling his belt and folding it in half. I'd feel that rush of fear, and my mouth would go dry. He'd beat me and forget all about Uncle Riccas and my Grandfather. I'll never forget the time my father got in a fight with Grand-daddy and hit him with a heavy-duty glass mug over his eye. I remember hearing them arguing in the basement, which was expected, and then the sound of furniture being moved around, a sure sign that someone was fighting in my house. Granddad started cursing and yelling,

"He cut my eye!"

The next thing I knew, my father came running up the steps and burst out the front door, my Uncle George on his heels, trying to catch him. Suddenly, Granddaddy appeared in the doorway with one hand pressed to the top of his eye. The blood was surging out with rhythm, seeping through his fingers and down his elbow. When he moved his hand away, I saw white tendons and bone.

My Grandma modestly yelled, *"What's going on? What's happening?"* My cousins came running. My Grandma called the ambulance and they took my Grandfather to the hospital. When the police came my Uncle George told them what happened. The police tried to find my father and couldn't. But three days later, Uncle Riccas figured out that my father was laying low with two junkies named Donald and Brenda, who lived in the projects. Riccas called the police on him. He went to jail for three months. My Grandfather was 70 years old when my father did this. He had an ugly scar above his eye for the rest of his life. After that incident, my grandfather never truly welcomed my father back into the house. Whatever little trust that existed was shattered, but Mama always vouched for him, Granddaddy would angrily and quietly walk away, harboring the weight of unspoken resentment.

One night, my Uncle Riccas broke both of my father's arms. Another time, my father almost killed Uncle Riccas with a cast-iron skillet. I remember my father on top of him, pounding his face repeatedly. He destroyed Uncle Riccas's face. When my father finally stood up, he was covered in blood, up to his elbows. I couldn't believe how much blood there was. It didn't even seem real. My father went to jail for that, too.

For the longest time, I never fought back because I feared that would only make it worse. Then, around age 10, I decided I'd had enough. My father came in, making lots of noise, mumbling, and cursing.

"Motherfuckin' bitches......."

He didn't say hello to anyone; he just went to the refrigerator and threw the door open so hard it smacked the wall. It must have been the beginning of the month because we had food. I remember him stooped over with a loaf of bread in his hand. I was already mad and irritated at his presence. Just look at him, eating our food. He didn't even live here. He made a sandwich and went to the kitchen table. As I watched him, my growing anger intensified. I had decided that this man was not my father. Long ago, he shattered my trust, and it became clear that his intentions were never about discipline; instead, he consistently sought to inflict harm upon me; he was always actively trying to hurt me.

"Little boy," he says, *"get me some water."*

I turned my head away in disgust. Was he crazy? The refrigerator was right behind him. I was in the dining room.

"Get your own water," I said.

He stiffened.

"What the fuck you say to me?"

I looked at my grandmother. She had a worried look on her face. This was the first time this had happened.

"Go get me some fucking water!" he shouted.

"Get your own water," I said.

He stood up, threw his plate against the wall, and came at me. I felt the familiar adrenaline rush, but I didn't wait this time. Once he got close, I started punching him. I hit him, and I didn't stop. I had been in so many fights in school I knew what to do. I learned to dodge and weave. Thanks to football, I could take a hit. He was punching at me, too, but he was missing. He might have hit me a few times, but I hit him a lot more.

49

Mama was screaming, *"Al, Al, stop!"* But both our names are Al. Then Uncle George came pounding up the steps from the basement. He picked me up and turned me around, putting his back to his brother because he knew my father wouldn't dare hit him. The only person my father wouldn't fight was my Uncle George, his older brother, because he knew he couldn't beat him. My Uncle George was the only *"normal"* person in our family. Having served in the military, he appeared to be the sole individual with a sensible grasp on life, morals, and some form of values.

"No, no, this shouldn't be happening," Uncle George said.

Uncle George; *"What are you doing?"*

"I don't give a fuck about him," my father shouted.

I quickly responded,

"Who cares, BITCH!"

He took off, flinging open the screen door and stomping down the steps. A moment later, he was halfway down the alley. Uncle George still had me in a bear hug, my feet off the ground. I was still struggling and flailing around.

"No, No, No," Mama kept saying.

Uncle George finally let me down. I raced upstairs to the room. I was so angry and hyped up; it took me a long time to settle down. A part of me felt terrible for fighting in front of my Grandma, but another part of me felt good. I could finally stop him from physically abusing me. It was an incredible feeling. I knew that part of my life was over.

It was only a few months later that Uncle George contracted pneumonia. He waited too long to go to hospital and died from complications. He was 41 years old. After that, my dad kept making verbal threats, trying to regain dominance. He wanted respect. He couldn't handle that his son wouldn't obey him. One day he threatened me and said he would kill me if I didn't obey.

"I put you on this earth, and I can take you out of it."

"I'll knock your brains out."

Looking back, I see he was frustrated with the world and would lash out at anyone he could in our family. After that first fight, I was always hurting him a lot more than he was hurting me. Each time we fought, I got a little better. By the time I was 12, he realized that he was never going to win, so he'd say things like,

"I don't fight you because I don't want to hurt you."

Around this time, I began to notice his addiction. Until then, I never understood that the drugs were driving his anger and rage. When he was out of jail, he found work as a car mechanic under Mr. Mike. It wasn't a trade he had studied in school; he was self-taught. Despite not having formal training, he possessed an extraordinary talent for fixing cars. Yet his struggles with addiction often clouded his judgment. Unfortunately, Mr. Mike took advantage of this, exploiting both his skills and his vulnerability. He would repair three or four cars daily, often with minimal assistance from Mr. Mike, who would reap the financial rewards. I only knew this because sometimes, I'd go to the shop with him and wash cars for money. I would watch their interactions. We'd be together all day and never speak. He would make sixty or eighty bucks a day, always under the table. We'd ride a hack (a freelance unauthorized ghetto taxi or Uber before Uber) home together, and he'd want to get out at the top of Norfolk but walk towards Hillsdale. He'd pay the driver and tell him to take me home, saying he had business. That's when I knew he was buying because that was a big drug area and the block all the main drug dealers sold on. Worse, it was embarrassing because many of the dealers were people I knew. I was thirteen, and most dealers were fifteen and sixteen. These were kids I saw in school or played youth football with.

We never had enough money to get through the month. It was expectedly unexpected that if my dad worked, he would give some of his money to Mama. However, even when he did, he always asked for it back.

"This boy needs food, Big Al," but his persistence wore her down. If she resisted, he would bide his time until she fell asleep, waking her up to inquire about the money's hiding place and reclaiming it. My grandma would be left with nothing from his previous contribution by morning. This became an unsettling and recurring cycle. I wouldn't say I liked it when he gave money to my grandmother because I knew it meant enduring the relentless back-and-forth throughout the night, making sleeping difficult, and constantly needing to keep one eye open. Witnessing him rummage through her mattress or go under her pillowcase to reclaim what he had given her made me sick and caused me not to have an appetite the next day.

"I'll pay you back tomorrow," he'd say, or *"I'll give you double tomorrow."* I must have heard that a million times. Mama would always give in to him; he never returned it. So I started taking and hiding the money from him so we could buy food to eat. He'd need a fix, then, in the middle of the night, he'd wake me up, asking for it, or come searching for it, saying it was an emergency. Night after night, he persisted in disrupting my sleep for school, repeatedly waking me up. I succumbed a few times due to fatigue and drowsiness. Eventually, he would find my hiding place; then, I'd have to find a new one, over and over again. Turning it into a cat-and-mouse game.

He developed strange habits because of his addiction. Since he did crack, he was obsessed with anything small and white. If you were sitting with him at a table and he saw something white, he would try to get it up with his finger. He'd realize it was just paint or something, yet he'd keep trying repeatedly. It was as if he wasn't in control of his mind, which I guess he wasn't. He would use drugs anywhere, even home. He became a hoarder, accumulating various useless and cumbersome items like old rims and car parts, scrap metal, and bed frames. These objects served as barricades for his bedroom door, a space he utilized for smoking crack. There was a day he went missing and no one could find him. I was looking for him everywhere and found him hiding in the closet. The burn marks inside the door from his lighter left a visual reminder of his addiction.

I learned how crack smelled. Crack smells like nothing else; it's a chemical smell like burning plastic. Now that I was understanding his addiction, things made more sense. I also noticed how his body would change. When he was using it, he would get really skinny and gaunt. When he was in jail or a psychiatric facility and eating three square meals a day, he would beef up, but after he'd come home, he'd start losing a lot of weight again. It happened over and over again. Before that, I never understood why he was always angry and wanted to fight. Especially me. However, now I saw that it had to do with the drugs, and the lost of a child. I didn't forgive him for it. I figured I should be more important to him than his drugs. Yet, deep down inside, I knew I wasn't. Nothing was.

"My father never taught me much of anything, but he indirectly taught me everything I didn't want to be because I didn't want to be like him." -Mayo-

"The reason I refrained from expressing or demonstrating love wasn't because I didn't love you. It was the fear of God taking you away, just like your sister, that held me back. For me, it was my method of safeguarding you. I've always loved you more than life itself, even more than God, until I truly understood who God really was. After your sister's death, I thought God was punishing me because of her demise,

so I dared not utter or exhibit anything that symbolized love. I'm not making excuses, but this is why I never dared to express the word 'love', fearing that God would take you too." - Alphonso Mayo Sr.-

CHAPTER *6*

GLORIOUS GLORIA

My first memory in life is that of my grandmother standing in the kitchen cleaning. She was constantly cleaning, and I later began to understand that was her way of coping and escaping the reality that was called our house, which was always in disarray. Similar to those fairytale movies, I looked up at her, and all I could remember seeing was a reflection of light beaming from her body. She didn't say anything as she stood there smiling at me. All I could do was smile and wonder why she was smiling at me. As an adult, I still wonder what she was thinking about? All I know is that Gloria Mayo was my hero, lifeline, world, angel, and heart outside of my body. She represented my depiction of genuine love. Yet, my family and community depicted something different, and that was a constant reminder of my reality.

"Grandmothers are the best; mothers are okay, but they are copycats of grandmothers. Every little boy loves his grandmother one notch above his mother because in the gentle embrace of a grandmother's love, the purest and most enduring bonds are woven." -Mayo-

It seemed our house was the community outreach center. We lived in an old row house, and most of our possessions could have been considered antiques because my family never purchased anything new. Whatever possessions they had from their previous life seem to move into existing times. However, our house wasn't a time capsule, more of a time bomb because of everyone's exploding temper, but not Mama.

When we lived on North Ave, the house was always dark, full of dull, dim light. Cigarette smoke always hung in the air, which stained the walls of the narrow hallways, and the smell was in everything. The cramped living conditions made me feel trapped. The old wooden floors always made a creaking and clanking sound. The refrigerator was always empty. Between the house pets and the overwhelming amount of roaches and mice, cleaning for my grandmother had to be a priority. Family friends would spend the night and even live with us for months at a time. The T.V.

was always on, often accompanied by one or two radios. Fans ran in the windows all summer long, and we spent countless hours out on the front stoop. Even within the community, everyone seemed to know one another.

In a sense, it was a close-knit community but shackled by the chains of poverty, dysfunction, crime, and miseducation. Amid the chaos, I wanted to believe that there was love among us, a bond that transcended our struggles. Yet, as time passed, it became clear that there was no love and even Mama's love alone couldn't mend the deep wounds of poverty and its accompanying behaviors. My Grandma, the matriarch of our family tried her best, but even her love and wisdom seemed powerless against the harsh realities we faced. Sadly, the people in our community appeared to be experiencing parallel lives, where each generation would repeat what was previously done.

My grandmother never seemed to be disturbed by any of it. Although she never said it openly, I could feel that she only wanted a loving family and her children to blossom. My grandmother had trouble keeping her children out of jail and out of the streets, but she still had a positive relationship with them. She never said "No" to our family or friends of family members who needed somewhere to stay, and she always did it with a smile and a big heart.

Everyone seemed to find their way back to my grandparent's home when things got tough for them. Many of my relatives lived with my grandmother for their entire lives, and she never demanded anything in return. Her actions were natural and sincere. I would not necessarily say I enjoyed it. Unfortunately, as I grew up, I felt that her spirit and sincere love prevented our family from growing. They took advantage of her kindness. There was very little repercussions for their actions. I always felt that she should have kicked them out or that my life would have been better if it were just me and my grandparents. When family fights erupted, she modestly said, *"Stop it!"* She never really screamed.

Fights between my Uncle and father started spontaneously—kind of out of the blue. I vividly remember this one fight when my grandmother was frying chicken in the kitchen. Before you knew it, they bumped into the stove, knocking the frying pot off, and the grease landed on my grandmother's leg. I was furious, but I was too small to do anything to protect her. She didn't even cry, and when she lifted her pant leg, her skin was gone. The deep burn on her dark-skin from the scalding hot grease left a red burn. I could see the pain on her face from her burning skin, but she said nothing. She never made a fuss. She didn't even kick them out or even call the police. She just went to the hospital and never said anything. I never understood how she could allow such behaviors. It made no sense to me.

I knew my grandmother was the rock of our family. She gave me the impression that everything would be fine and that everything would work out. Even with the chaos, Grandma always made it seem as if I was supposed to do something special with my life. She never said it aloud, but her eyes said, ***"Get out of this mess, Little Al."*** My connection to my Grandma was special. When you're young, you take many things for granted. I know I did. Today, as I reflect, when she was standing in the kitchen looking at me smiling, maybe it was her way of apologizing in advance because she knew she had no control over our lives. She didn't clean up because our house was messed up; she cleaned up because our lives were messed up, and that was the only time she felt a sense of control.

"You cannot control what happens to you, but you can control your attitude toward what happens to you, and in that, you will be mastering change rather than allowing it to master you." -Brian Tracy-

CHAPTER 7

HIS HEART IS BROKEN

I fell in love with football when I was six. The first time I saw Barry Sanders, I was amazed. I wanted to be that good, and I started practicing that same day, just on my own. I would run through the alleys, dodging, spinning, and working on my moves. When we played tag, I imagined I was Barry, #20, channeling his powers, and no one could touch me. After playing football with the other kids, my chest would often hurt, but I thought it was because I was tired. None of the other kids could stop me, but something bigger was about to happen.

Later that year, the holes in my heart began to widen. I didn't understand what was happening at the time; I just started having chest pains. At first, I didn't feel comfortable telling anyone in my family. It got to the point where the chest pain became unbearable. I was short of breath and constantly dizzy. I told my Grandma, and she took me to the University of Maryland Hospital. They did an EKG and immediately noticed that my irregular heartbeat had been worsening. They did more tests, including a C.T. scan. I was worried, but no one was telling me anything. I was seven years old. Mama said I would need surgery, but I didn't understand what that meant. She made it sound like it was no big deal as usual. A few weeks later, I went back to the hospital, still having chest pain. But by now, I've learned what heart surgery was. I knew the doctors would "cut" me, and the surgery could kill me.

I remember sitting in the waiting room. The longer we waited, the more anxious I became. Every time the nurse came and called someone back, I would freeze up. After the fifth time, I was utterly terrified. I was looking at the door and waiting to hear my name. I was a wreck, and I'd convince myself these were my last minutes on earth. The only thing that kept me from running away was my Grandma. She seemed so relaxed, and that reassured me.

Finally, we were called back to talk to a counselor. I didn't understand what he was talking about. Grandma said yes to everything.

"Yes."

"Yes."

"Yes."

"Yes."

They took me to another room, asking me to remove my clothes and put on a gown. My Grandma tied it up in the back. Doctors and nurses kept coming in. Then the surgeon and his team came and introduced themselves.

"You're a strong young boy," the surgeon said.

"Everything will be fine." You won't feel anything."

Even though he said that I didn't feel reassured, all these people with all this equipment, I could tell that this was serious.

Soon enough, I was lying on the gurney, and they were wheeling me down the hall. I'm clutching with all my might to my grandmother's hand. I didn't say anything, but weirdly I thought,

"If I die, God, protect her."

We arrived in the operating room, and they asked me to wear a mask similar to what older adults use for oxygen.

"Breathe for me," the anesthesiologist said. *"Take a deep breath."*

I could hear my Grandma saying,

"I love you."

She still sounded calm, so I took a deep breath. The next thing I remembered was waking up and seeing my mother. I opened my eyes, and this beautiful African American woman was leaning over me, smiling.

"Hey, sweetie, it's Mommy. I've brought you something to keep you company."

Until then, I had never seen my biological mother and was happy she was there. She held up a brown panda bear and tucked it under my arm, then gave me a warm smile and ran her hand down my cheek.

"Everything is going to be okay, sweetie. Remember, Mommy loves you."

And then I fell back asleep. When I awoke again, I was in great pain. Everything was blurry, like someone had smudged my eyes. Someone had brought me balloons, but my vision was so bad I couldn't see their outlines. I kept blinking until my eyes finally adjusted. I tried to say something, but I couldn't. My throat was painfully dry. I tried to sit up, and no matter how hard I tried, I couldn't. I looked around, and that's when I heard the nurse say, *"He's awake."* A minute later, my Grandma was beside me, kissing me. I figured she must have been waiting for me a long time because her breath smelled awful. But I could see the look of relief on her face. The skin on my chest felt tight, and it was all covered in bandages. I had an IV in my arm and a catheter in my penis. I couldn't even go to the bathroom alone.

I was in the hospital for ten days. My Grandma, Uncle George, and some of my cousins would come to see me. My dad never came. Those hospital days were long; I would lose track of time. After four or five days, I started getting up, walking and playing in the halls. By the end of it, I was running around and causing the nurses all kinds of trouble.

I waited for my mom to return, and I took the brown panda bear with me everywhere. I kept asking my Grandma where she was; she always seemed confused about the question. I kept imagining that I would see her and catch a glimpse of her in the hallway or down past the nurses' station. I would call her, but it was never her.

Grandma: *"Al, what are you talking about?"*

Me: *"My mother, she came to see me. Is she coming back?"*

Grandma: *"Al, please rest."*

When I finally went home, most of my family was waiting for me. They had put together a welcome home celebration with some balloons, music, and food. Everyone seemed excited to see me, but all I could think about was my mom. Why would she give me the bear and not come back? It didn't make sense. Did she know about the party? Why wasn't she here? I turned to my Grandma and said, "Why doesn't she want me?" She told me to enjoy the party, but I couldn't.

Over the years, the bear became my most prized possession. I named him David because I had once heard about a character from the bible who had a heart for God. I figured since I had a heart for my mom, I would name the bear she gave me after him. I kept it safe and slept with it for years. Then, it became filthy, so I tried to wash and blow dry it once, making the ears and nose wrinkle and fall off. After many years of kicking it around it was beat up, but I refused to get rid of David because he connected me to my mom. I must have spent the first seven years of my life just thinking about my mother. Questions like,

"Why did she leave me?"

"Why wasn't I worthy of her love?

"Does she think about me?"

"Does she ask about me?"

I thought we would reconnect by her coming to see me, but all it did was break my heart. Her absence went on for years. In seventh grade, I would ride the city bus and study all the women who looked about my mother's age. I would look into each of their faces and search for things that seemed familiar—the shape of the lips, the curve of the nose—looking for a family resemblance. And I would wonder if this woman or that woman was my mother. Then I'd fantasize about impossible things, stupid things that I knew could never come true. Things like her recognize me, that she'd apologize for leaving me, and that she'd take me away from the miserable life I had.

"My desire to exit the game is greater than my desire to remain in it. I have searched my heart through and through and feel comfortable with this decision."-Barry Sanders-

I've always felt that my mother's desire to exit my life was more significant than her desire to remain in it. I've searched my heart through and through, and I've always been uncomfortable with not being wanted. I've always been uncomfortable with being born and not being cared for. I've always been uncomfortable with feelings of emptiness because of the love I desired from her. On the day that I decided to throw the panda bear away I realized that she never cared about me at all.

"Why did I come out from the womb to see toil and sorrow, and spend my days in shame?" Jeremiah 20:18

CHAPTER 8 BACK STORY

HE'S DIFFERENT: UNCLE GEORGE

During my freshman year at Stevenson University, I wrote a story about my uncle in creative writing. It was a four-page essay that I never expected to see again. Today, I'm not sure where the essay is. However, it is one of the driving factors for *"The Promise."* It wouldn't have been an option had Mr. B not asked me to write my story. I'm going to do everything in my power to recapture this moment. I am unsure if it's possible because I was in a different space then. I was writing from a place of pain and sadness. I remember writing the essay and feeling every moment, crying throughout, trying to catch every detail. Now, I'm attempting to do the same here.

HE'S DIFFERENT: UNCLE GEORGE

He never said much, and something about his spirit was different. He wasn't a fighter, but he was a protector. He was not a big man. He stood at 5 foot 9 and looked just like World Wrestling Federation "WWF" wrestler Mark Henry. No one said anything, but everyone in my family respected him. He had no children, but would discipline every child in our house if something went wrong. There was a norm that if one of us did something wrong, we would all be disciplined to learn from each other's mistakes. He also carried himself like that among my older family members. He never let anybody disrespect my grandparents when he was around, but he was never around enough. My dad and Uncle Riccas were afraid of him—a bonus for me.

We rarely talked, and we weren't as close as my Grandma and I, but I knew I could trust him. I knew he loved me, though he never said it. When he was home, I observed him and how he interacted with various people within my family. It wasn't mentioned, but he was an alpha male, and I always viewed him as a father. I don't know what kind of work he did, but I knew he brought a smile to my grandparents' faces. That was rare, and it meant so much to me because I wanted to do the same thing when I grew up. He was just different.

There's a knock on the door from the neighbor. The door opened, and there stood a lady requesting to speak to my grandmother. I can hear the urgency in her voice.

"Is Ms. Gloria at home? I need to talk to her immediately."

"Hi, Ms. Gloria, the hospital is on the telephone, and they need to talk to you right away."

My grandma, always in the kitchen, comes out the door with a panicked look. I knew something wasn't right because she always had a calm attitude and demeanor, but this time it was different. I was standing in the dining room playing with an etch a sketch. Soon afterward, the door opens, and it's my grandmother. The look on her face told me she was hurt to the core. The look in her eyes was not fear. It was not that of sadness. I had seen this look from other people, but never from my grandma. It was the look of brokenness and hopelessness. She looked as if she had heard the news that someone had died. She stepped in, and everything seemed heavy. I could see the tears in her eyes. She looked at me slightly, gave me a half-smile, and pretended to be alright. She called my grandfather.

"George, come here, please."

Grandma: *"He's gone."*

Granddaddy: *"Who's gone, Gloria?"*

Grandma: *"George is gone!"*

I knew that whatever had happened was bad because neither my grandfather nor my grandmother ever cried, at least in front of me. As much as I wanted to hold it in, I erupted with emotions. The protector is "gone." My etch a sketch wet, covered with tears as I sat there.

A few days prior, I was in the same spot playing with the same etch a sketch when my uncle walked past me, and his mouth was filled with blood. Sweat ran down his face as he leaned over and spat it out. He looks at me and he says,

"I'm okay. Don't worry; I'll be okay."

"I'm going to go to the hospital."

I didn't think anything of it because this was my Mark Henry, my strongest man in the world, my protector, the person that made my grandparents smile, so I trusted him. He turns to my Grandma and says,

"I think I need to go to the hospital."

My grandfather, in agreement, nods his head. My grandmother does the same and says, ***"Yes, you should go."*** My family never went to the hospital. In my young observation, the males in my family never went to the hospital. I never imagined that would be my last encounter with Uncle George, but it was. My uncle died March 30th, 1997. He was 41 years old.

My Uncle George was everything my dad wasn't. He earned respect because he gave respect. Once I got into a fight with a girl who spat in my face. In response, I punched her in the eye. My Uncle George had unspoken rules, and if you broke those rules, it came with severe consequences. My uncle disapproved and ended up kicking my ass for it. For example, young men do not hit young women no matter what. How was I supposed to know that? I was always fighting with my girl cousins, but I learned that day. My uncle taught me how to ride a bike. My uncle took me on my first train/subway ride, showing me the entire city and how it connects to the county. When our dining room ceiling leaked, I watched my uncle fix it. When my mother abandoned me, my uncle came to get me from that basement on Division Street. I could never repay him for that, I could never replace that, and worse still, I never got to say thank you.

I stopped caring for David; he became just another teddy bear to kick around. He became a source of frustration because every time I looked at him, my heart broke because I knew my mother didn't love me and I would probably never see her. One of the biggest regrets of my life is that I fixated on people who didn't love me instead of cherishing those who did.

In July of 2006, almost 10 years later, I was cleaning and trashing things, preparing for college. It was David's turn to be placed in the garbage. Until that moment, I had never noticed that the inside of the tag was signed. Although faded, it read from *"Uncle George."*

It all started to make sense. My mother had never visited me in the hospital, just the yearning of a broken little boy. I felt so awful because I had wasted so much energy on someone who didn't care about me when I had someone who loved me—Uncle George— and I never showed him how much I loved him as I should have.

The same is true for my grandma. In her, I had a much better mother than many children. Yet, I had been too fixated on my biological mother to see and appreciate it. My regret is magnified tenfold by the fact that he died before I realized the truth, before I could tell him how important he was to me and how he inspired me to break out of the cycle I was in. He'll never know how much I needed him or the nights I spent in fear, wishing he was there to say something and protect me.

During my freshman year at North Carolina Central University, I ran around the track every night for hours, listening to T.I. - Live In The Sky, thinking about him and how I needed his guidance. I reflected on how I defied the odds and wished he could have witnessed my accomplishments. Praying that he was proud of me and because I was hundreds of miles away from my grandparents, praying his spirit would watch over and protect them. My uncle imparted valuable lessons that I've embraced now as a man. It's just unfortunate that I didn't get the chance to show him in time.

Thank you, Uncle George, for being a father to me. For loving me and disciplining me. I'm not at all where I desire to be, nor am I the man you were, but I'm doing my best to make you proud.

"Every little boy's first superhero is their father; for me, it was my Uncle George." -Mayo-

CHAPTER 9

YOU'RE CUT

Violence, hostility, peril—they all hung in the air like an invisible mist. You couldn't see it, but you sensed it in the streets, at school, and at home. Making everything tense and precarious. You could see it on the sidewalks, in how the women held their bags close and checked over their shoulders. You could see it in the eyes of women as the corner boys approached them. You could see it in the rugged looks of the boys at the corner, constantly assessing if you were a friend or foe. You felt it in the laughter of the dealers; their hearty guffaws veined with violence. I smelled it in the burnt plastic smell of crack in my house and the smelly odor similar to rotten garlic with a hint of turnip that my grandfather described as "marijuana" in the community airs. Lastly, you could see it in the wobbling zombie walk of the junkies.

This is a zero-sum game. Whatever you have that is good and precious, beware. Someone is willing and ultimately thinking about taking it from you, including your life. So you learn to be hard. You learn to hide your feelings. You know not to cry or show that anything hurts. Day after day, you learn the life lessons of what living in poverty wants you to learn. The inevitable teachings of the street, deprivation, and stress. You start to believe and embrace the mindset that you will not amount to much. I remember feeling this at a very young age. With no knowledge of statistics or probabilities. Without understanding poverty, social class, incarceration rates, or early death. Yet, I still knew that I was very small in this world, my opportunities were limited, and no one was coming to save me, especially not my mother and father.

When I was little, I lived in fear. I feared that my father would abuse me and our family's brutal fights. I feared the sounds of gunshots and that one day I would be killed. I feared walking to and from school and getting jumped. I feared being called on by my teacher in class to read aloud and being picked on for not possessing the same abilities as my classmates. I feared that I would never see my mother again and most of all that I would never escape the fear. Over time I started to cope with my fears by not caring what the outcomes were.

From as early as I can remember, well into my teen years, I was trying to navigate my world while living with PTSD. *"Post-traumatic stress disorder (PTSD) develops in response to exposure to a traumatic event during which an individual feels extremely fearful, horrified, or helpless. The diagnosis is characterized by persistent re-experiencing of the event, persistent avoidance of stimuli associated with the event, emotional numbing, and hyper-arousal (APA, 1994)."* The only person I did not fear was my grandmother. She was the only one who believed in me.

We moved to South Baltimore to the Cherry Hill Community. Even though our new home was six miles away, it felt like we were far removed from all the pain, hurt, abuse, and fear that I had experienced living on North Avenue. I was happy, excited, and curious. The 13-minute drive to the house felt like hours and made me anxious. We pulled in front of an all-brick, end-of-group townhome with an enclosed front porch and fenced backyard. I stayed outside taken by the beauty of the house. Goodbye stoop, goodbye corner boys, goodbye fear as I walked directly across the street to the local park. Unlike our home on North Avenue, it was more relaxed. It was me, my grandparents, Aunt Teresa, Uncle George, and Uncle Riccas, that all filled the space.

I couldn't contain my curiosity, so I didn't sleep much the first night. The following day, I decided to walk around the community. Within minutes, I met this tall, skinny kid named Mike. We were the same age, but he was twice my height.

"Yo, what's your name?"

Me: "Little Al"

"Did you just move around here?"

Me: "Yeah, yesterday."

"Do you play football?"

Me: "Yeah"

"Come with us."

We walked a few blocks away to this big field to play football without asking for permission. This became a daily routine, and Mike became my football friend. I would join pickup games after school and mess up my clothes. I wasn't supposed to. It had only been a little over two years since I had heart surgery, and the doctors had told my grandma that playing competitive sports could kill me. But I didn't care. I was having too much fun. Football became my escape from reality. Even though we had moved, the traumas of my past still haunted me. However, on the field I found release. The game provided a sanctuary where I could momentarily forget my problems and just be free.

We would play in the alleys, with the row houses on both sides and glass-covered cement under our feet. The softest thing you could land on was a plastic trash can. It was excellent motivation not to get tackled. When the season started, Mike convinced me to play for the rec league team, the Cherry Hill Chiefs. I knew I shouldn't, but I couldn't let it go. So, I went to the first team meeting and forged my grandma's signature.

Everything seemed to be falling into place—until it was time to pay. I just needed $90, a seemingly small amount, yet so out of reach. I knew I couldn't turn to my father for help. Our relationship was strained, to say the least. Summoning all my courage, I approached him, plastering a forced smile on my face, pretending that everything was okay between us. I spoke to him as politely as I could, hoping this time would be different. I needed just $9 from him, everyday for the next ten days, to make up the total. It was a small request, or so I thought. But as always, I was disappointed. Even the simplest request seemed to trouble him. He never gave me the money. He told Mama to give it to me. Immediately, she started to question why I needed the money. She became increasingly persistent, eventually extracting the answer from me. Worry etched across her face, and tears welled up as she expressed the fear that I could die.

"You can die, Lil Al. Is that what you want?"

I felt bad. She kept repeating what the doctor said—absolutely no competitive sports. But honestly, I figured that dying playing sports would be better than growing up with my family. Strangely, on this occasion, Big Al was pushing for me. I don't know why because he never advocated for me or even talked to my grandma about me. *"Let him play,"* he said. *"Everything will be fine."* Grandma shook her head, repeating what the doctor had said. *"He won't get hurt,"* my dad insisted, *"It's just little kids."* Mama kept looking at me while he talked. My dad would say something, and she'd look at me and shake her head, and that's how the conversation ended. I went to our room, knowing my chances of playing football were over. I was disappointed, but I knew she would find out eventually anyway and make me quit. When I got home from school the next day, Mama was cleaning up like usual. I went to our room and when I got to the bottom of the steps she handed me the signed parent waiver and ninety dollars in cash. She said nothing. Her face was devoid of expression.

I tried to hide my excitement, but I went right out the door and ran as fast as I could up to the recreation center to turn it all in. I practiced with the team for the next three days, but we had a new Head Coach on the fourth day. On his first day, he began cutting kids without watching them play. He had us line up, and he just went down the line.

"You cut," yes you, *"You cut."*

Loud as if to embarrass each player.

"You Cut!"

One by one, each player would bow his head and walk off the field. It was so unfair because it was based on who he already knew.

"You cut. You cut."

Right on down the line. Then he came up to me. He didn't know me and had never seen me play. *"You cut,"* he said. I felt a trickle of shock run down my back. They were just words, but I was devastated. I bowed my head like all the other kids and began walking away. I wanted to play because I understood the release that came with the sport. It was more than just a game; it was my relief. I loved the exhilaration that came with performing well. It was my way of breaking free from my circumstances. And then there was the money. The $90 was non-refundable. I knew it was a significant amount for Mama to give, and I couldn't bear the thought of telling her.

Teammate: *"Hold on, coach."*

Coach: *"What is It?"*

Teammate: *"He's good; you gotta keep him."*

Teammate: *"Keep him; you'll see."*

The other kids were sticking up for me. That meant so much to me, especially one kid who played the same position as me because keeping me meant he'd play less. That was one of the few times people had stood up for me in my childhood. I didn't have brothers, but it was my first taste of the brotherhood I would find on the football field.

We did well. I played well and I had many great teammates. We went to the POT 1 championship. Even though we lost to the Eastern Wood Ravens, I knew I had enormously contributed to my team. No one from my family came to any of my games, but I was happy that I did something the doctors said I couldn't do. More importantly, I was stronger and learning to overcome the pain of being "abandoned."

You're cut; it feels like you're rejected, not wanted, not loved, and being abandoned. -Mayo-

CHAPTER *10*

MONEY – WE NEVER HAD ENOUGH

There's being poor, and then there's being Black. When you come from where I come from, both make you self-conscious. You feel that people are always looking down on you. Combined seems to be a bad combination and weighs on you heavily psychologically.

We didn't talk much about money or how it worked. We never spoke much as a family. I never asked questions, and most of my learning in my early years was done through observation. On the first of the month, I noticed my family members' moods change because they seemed calmer and more optimistic. That quickly changed a few days later. Then, there was chaos again. That was the routine for my first 16 or 17 years. I was unaware I was on a social and economic roller coaster that appeared to have no end.

Although we had it bad, I always felt like my grandmother had it worse. She would let the whole family eat first, then eat whatever was left. If there were ten pieces of chicken, she would wait until only one wing or thigh was left and that would be all she would eat. Some nights, I witness her not getting anything. I'd ask her if she wanted some of my food, and she would say no, claiming she had already eaten and was full, but I knew it wasn't true. Later, I'd see granddaddy in the kitchen eating spam or little Vienna sausages he liked. It used to bother me because I knew I couldn't do anything about it. I knew I couldn't ask my family questions, but I always wondered why they didn't do anything. Do they not see what my young eyes see? It hurt so much knowing my grandparents were suffering.

My granddad's pension was around $975. I will always remember that number. That's what we had to live on, and most of it went towards rent. We got food stamps because of the five children in the house. Now, with all those kids getting food stamps, you'd think we'd have enough to eat, but we didn't. I rarely had breakfast at home. I'd eat lunch at school but wouldn't say I liked the food there. I had no choice but to learn to love it. It was a badge of shame because only the poorest kids ate it. As for dinner, sometimes I ate, and sometimes I didn't.

Around the 11th or 12th, we ran out of food. I'd open the fridge, and there'd be a few eggs, bread ends, and canned milk. Until we would get more food, I'd eat cereal with water and syrup sandwiches. King Syrup was my favorite. I also would eat Oodles of Noodles over and over, chicken pack, oriental pack, or beef pack. The beef pack was the best. Eventually, there would be no more of that. So I didn't eat, or I ate junk food for the rest of the month.

In the last week of the month, we just had to hope some money trickled in. Uncle Riccas never worked, but he would go out and collect cans. It would bring in $15 or $30, and he would give half of it to my grandmother to buy more chicken and Oodles of Noodles. If Uncle Riccas had a good day, we might get chicken—otherwise, more noodles. As previously mentioned, if my father weren't incarcerated, he would occasionally do odd jobs at Mr. Mike's garage, earning some money. However, a significant portion of his earnings typically went towards supporting his crack habit. Now and then, he would hand over around $20 or $30 to my grandma for food. However, by the night's end, he would ask for it back.

When the first of the month finally came, I was the happiest kid in the world because I knew I would eat again. We would shop at the cheapest places: Food City, Farm Fresh, and Stop, Shop, and Save. They were filthy, and you had to check the packages carefully for rat and mice bites, especially at Food City. I remember getting some bread home and finding rats had partially eaten it. We didn't have a car, so it was only on the first of the month that we would splurge and take a hack home from the market. After that, if you needed food, you had to find something close to the house. Going to the store was like a fantasy but often short-lived, as I knew there would never be enough to hold us over.

Interestingly, the first few days of the month, I could see my family's potential. I was able to sense what it would be like if we had constant financial resources and if we could always afford to buy food consistently. Not only did I see it, but I was able to feel an abundance of joy with my family, knowing there was an active source of resources in the home. There were no concerns that our income was government assistance. It made me feel like if we didn't have all these financial challenges, my life could be different. However, I was aware that this fantasy would not last long and that people would eventually return to their regular routines, which was my reality. I realized that my family's hope would ultimately turn to hopelessness, as that was the only way they knew how to cope with chaos. Unfortunately, we never had enough money, food, peace, joy, love, or conversation.

As I got older, when there wasn't any food in the house, I did what I felt was necessary. Selling drugs wasn't an option, but hustling was. I found unique ways to earn money to give to my grandmother without anybody in my family knowing. First, I imitated my Uncle Riccas by picking up cans and walking them from my house on Violet Avenue down to the scrap yard on Pennsylvania Avenue. It was a 2.7-mile walk from my house, but fortunately, it was a straight shot. Before then, I had asked my Uncle if I could help him carry the cans to the scrap yard only to get a sense of direction.

Hundreds of cans for about $10. Didn't make a whole lot of money, cents, or sense. So, I started going to Mr. Mike's shop with my father to wash cars on the weekends, netting around $20-$40. It may not have been much, but it was certainly better than nothing. I couldn't wait until it snowed because that's when I had the most significant financial impact in supporting my grandmother and, indirectly, my family. I had a clientele of 25 houses that paid me between $10 and $20 to shovel their sidewalks, driveways, and clean off their car. I did it myself in my early years. As my younger cousins got older, I began to take them with me and give them a percentage of our profits. I earned $200-$400 every time, depending on how much snow fell and how many clients needed services. I would go home and give every dime I had to my grandmother. I wouldn't say anything; I would hand it to her, walk away and smile silently.

Before my hustling days, I'd show up at a friend's house around dinner time, hoping to eat with them. That's when I saw how ordinary people lived. They didn't fight over food, hoard it in their rooms, or eat it as fast as they could because they knew if they didn't, someone else would. Although others in my house stashed food, I never did. It was always so little. If I had extra food, I would eat it immediately. You risked losing it to other people, mice, and roaches if you stashed it.

What is it like to be hungry day after day? Have you ever left your house in the morning and realized you forgot something important? Then you find out you have a flat tire? On top of that, you drop your phone, and it breaks? It's the feeling that the world is against you and nothing is going your way. That's how you feel when you are not eating enough. Everything is a struggle; you are always irritated, constantly short-tempered, and angry. It becomes part of your identity. This contributed to my fighting. But I got used to it. Since it happened every month, this became my norm.

When I was thirteen or fourteen, I went to the store with Mama. I would always ask Mama, *"Did you check the card?"* To receive food stamps, you had to submit paperwork every six months. If you didn't, they canceled the monthly SNAP benefits on your card. I always asked Mama to confirm the balance by phone before we made the trip to the store.

"Don't worry," she said. *"I checked it."*

We got there, and she got out her list. I don't know why, because we always bought the same thing. White bread at 99 cents. Frosted Flakes, Cornflakes, Oodles of Noodles, and spaghetti. Then, for the meats, sodium-free ham, spam cans, tons of chicken, hotdogs, ground beef, milk, and Kool-aid. "Rich Food" was the store brand and cheapest, so we purchased that. Every other month, she'd try to do something nice, like buy a steak, but she didn't know how to cook it.

As we filled the cart, my mouth was watering, and my stomach was growling. I can't wait to get home and finally eat. We went through every aisle, and the cart was full, with a massive mound on top. We must have waited in line for an hour because the store was crowded. It's the first of the month, everyone is at the store, buying food with food stamps. Yet, despite the shared experience, I can't shake off the feelings of insecurity and shame. It's as if the eyes of others are fixed directly on us, magnifying our inadequacies and shortcomings. Finally, we load up the belt and run it all through. The total amount is about $320. Grandma swipes her food stamps card.

"Ma'am, your card didn't go through," the cashier says.

"Oh, can I do it again?"

She swiped it. Still didn't work. She tried again.

"Nope."

I stood there looking at her, and I was so disgusted. I was so angry that she hadn't checked. There we were with all our food in bags, ready to go, and we had no choice but to leave it there. It was humiliating. Everyone was staring at us. I couldn't even look at grandma. I walked in front of her. We caught the hack back home, my stomach squeezing in on itself with hunger. That experience taught me an important lesson: I cannot tolerate being embarrassed, and being on welfare and government assistance was fucking humiliating.

Looking back, I could see that this moment of embarrassment drove a lot of my behavior. If the teacher asked me to read in front of the class, I would lash out, get up and leave. I couldn't let anyone know that I didn't know how to read. It was the same with fighting. If someone threatened or made me uncomfortable, I'd hit them. Even if their true intentions weren't to fight, I wasn't going to allow them to embarrass me.

I told myself that I never wanted to be on government assistance for any reason. Although the card my grandmother used said *"Independence card,"* to me, there was nothing independent about utilizing food stamps. That moment didn't sit right with me. I knew we wouldn't be in this position if my family worked for it. Yet, no one was striving to work for it, and it was the same routine every month. The feeling of never having enough eventually became a sense that you'll never be enough.

Observing my family throughout my childhood helped me understand a few realizations. Government assistance programs like food stamps and public housing aren't a way out. Having that mindset was nothing more than a trap, as it could make you overly dependent. I knew people needed it, but I always figured people should try to make it temporary. Use it as mobility, not stability, to break free from a demeaning system.

"I didn't say it to him, but I said it in front of him so he could hear. I said, "I fuckin' hate being poor." And my dad got upset. He didn't scream or howl. That wasn't his way. He just threw his newspaper on the floor and said, "David, David, David. You are not poor." He said, "Poor is a mentality." He said, "It's a mentality that very few people ever recover from. Don't you forget it, son. You are broke." He said, "These are just financial circumstances that I hope to overcome one day very soon." And I said, "Well, Dad, whatever you want to call this, uh, it's wildly uncomfortable." -Dave Chappelle-

CHAPTER *11*
RUNNING FOR MY LIFE

As I stated in a previous chapter, the team did well in my first year of recreational football, and I knew I had made an enormous contribution to my team. From my point of view, I knew that I was sacrificing more than my teammates could imagine. At the end of the season, they gave me a small trophy the size of my hand during the awards banquet. It struck me as strange—was this supposed to symbolize all my hard work? All the work in the summer, facing the process of being cut, and risking my life. I trashed it because I knew it wasn't indicative of my play or ability.

When I turned 11, we moved to Violet Avenue in Northwest Baltimore, and I joined the Park Heights Spartans. Their colors were white and green, like Michigan State. Coach Larry was the first full-fledged coach I ever had. He knew football and mentored his players. It was weird how our relationship started. I was walking home from school, and a car pulled up.

Coach Larry: *"Hey, you play ball?"*

Me: *"I did, but we just moved around here."*

Coach Larry: *"You walk like a running back."* *"My name is Coach Larry; what's yours?"*

Me: *"Lil Al."*

Coach Larry: *"You think you can run the ball for me?"*

That was all I needed to hear. He came to my house, met my grandma, and offered to drive me to practice. When he couldn't give me a ride, I ran and sometimes walked 2.5 miles to practice. No big deal. When I would walk, I would observe my surroundings and think,

"This shit can't be life."

I played tailback and fullback for most of my youth years. In our first game, we played The First and Ten Cowboys at Northwestern High School, which would later become the high school I attended. I scored five touchdowns that game.

Every game after that I scored two to three touchdowns per game. This was Pop Warner football, and they had weight limits. I had to be weighed twice for every game because the coaches from the other teams would argue that I was too big or that I must be older, but I wasn't. Against the Gardenville Gators, I weighed in at 136 lbs. The maximum weight for the age group 8-10 was 135lbs. One pound over, and they wouldn't let me play. I remember thinking how unfair it was. We lost the game but would have won if I played.

We went to the playoffs that year, but we lost. I was a proud kid and knew how important I was to my team. Even though I missed that one game, I still had twenty-plus touchdowns. So I felt a little cheated when they gave the MVP to a kid named Dante Stuckey, who played quarterback. Coach Larry wasn't the head coach, but I was under the impression that he betrayed me. I worked hard for him and felt he didn't fight for me. I considered playing for a different team but was loyal to Coach Larry. Later, I learned that he was also upset by the decision, and before the next season started, coach Larry retired.

The following year, the coaches asked me to skip several brackets to play in the oldest age bracket, eleven to fourteen-year-olds, Under Coach Barnes. We weren't a good team, and the players weren't committed. The parents did not come to the games, and every other day, a player quit. I was playing hard, and yet, we were losing. Finally, Coach Barnes decided to fold the team and cancel the season. He pulled me aside to tell me he wanted me to continue playing ball.

Coach Barnes: *"Phonso, come here."*

Me: *"Yes, Sir."*

Coach Barnes: *"Look, this season is not going well, and you're a great player. I'm sending you to my son."*

Me: *"No, Sir, I'm not going to quit. We can play with who we have."*

Coach Barnes: *"Son, listen to me; it's over. He's the Coach of the Northwest Bulldogs. His name is D.J. You'll love him."*

Me: *"Yes, Sir."*

I played for the Northwest Bulldogs under Coach D.J. Barnes. He had a great program that was well organized, with many dedicated football moms. And it was much tougher competition. I realized I hadn't been working that hard. Coach D.J. was a different kind of coach. Long cornrows and an intense voice like the rapper DMX, big and deep, and when he spoke, you listened. He was like a motivational speaker. He worked us hard and kept us late. He'd have the parents drive their cars onto the field and turn on the lights so we could practice in the dark. We dominated the league.

There was only one team in the league we couldn't beat, the Northwood Rams. We lost to them in the regular season and had to play them in the City Championship. They defeated us 6-0. I'll never forget it; they ran a toss play to this kid named Disco. Who ran from sideline to sideline, back and forth, trying to find a hole to break through. Eventually, he found one opening and scored. That was a tough loss because they went on to win the National Championship in Florida. Just thinking about it today gives me a sick feeling in my stomach. If we could have beaten them, that could have been us. I remember they played R. Kelly's "I Wish" as our come-out song. Every time I hear that song, I get that same sick feeling.

I wasn't named our team's MVP that year, but I was proud of myself because I didn't feel like I deserved it, despite knowing as a player I was good and contributed to my team's success. Ultimately, we were a great team. After transferring from the Spartans, I arrived late in the season and earned playing time and my teammates' respect. This alone was gratifying. Although they were like brothers, I was an outsider. Yet, they took me in and taught me to work hard and earn playing time.

I moved to the eleven-fourteen brackets under Coach Roland Brown the following year. Roland was fat and seemingly lazy, but, hands down, he was the best coach I have ever had on any level, including college. He was massive, with a big bald head and a thin goatee. He would get an ice cream cone and say, *"Ya'll run until I finish my ice cream."* Most people can finish an ice cream cone in five to ten minutes tops, but Coach Roland could make that ice cream last 25 minutes. His tongue must have been made of ice because it never seemed to melt. His philosophy was simple.

"Do what I tell you to do when I ask you to do it, and everything will be fine."

He didn't play favorites; the best person in a position was on the field. If you started messing up, you'd get pulled and have to fight for your spot back. This was a big team with three full squads, so you always had to fight to keep your position.

In addition to being a great coach, Coach Roland became a surrogate father to me, something I truly needed. He was someone who was tough, level-headed, and fair. He was rational and thoughtful while taking a sincere interest in the kids he coached. In other words, he was the opposite of my biological father. In my second year, I couldn't afford to play; he just said, "Don't worry about it." He bought all the players' gear, including socks, undershirts, jockstraps, and cups. That inspired us. We felt we owed him, so we would work as hard as possible.

He made a big difference in my discipline. He taught us to behave more like men, whatever that means. We weren't allowed to talk back to him. When he gave us an order, we had to say, *"Yes, sir,"* and *"No, sir."* We could have an opinion, but we had to tell him one-on-one; we couldn't and were not allowed to do it in front of the team. Another plus was that he would sometimes provide us with dinner. You could show up at his house any time, and he would give you food, and if you wanted to stay the night, you were welcome. I went to his house all the time during the season. I felt a strong sense of security around him, that even if I made a mistake, he would listen and wouldn't judge me. It's because he led by example. If he made a mistake in his coaching, and we lost, he would take responsibility. I'd never seen anyone in my family do that. But I saw the importance of that honesty and began to emulate it. We won eleven games and made it to the city championships but lost to Loch Raven.

Coach Roland was the man, and I believed whatever he told us because I could see the results. He gave such a powerful speech that made an impression on me as a young man and I still carry many of the lessons with me today.

"Fellas, do you know what makes a great player?"

"Anybody can play for a good team; anyone can just be part of a good team and win. That doesn't make him great; that makes him average and good at best."

"Fellas, what makes a great player is playing for a team with no hope, all while giving them hope. Inspiring other players around them to play above average and believe in their greatness. Fellas, that's what makes a great player."

"You have to decide who you're willing to become."

"You must decide if you'll be great or just average."

"Do you understand?"

In one accord, all the players yelled, *"Yes, Sir."*

My last year of eligibility for youth football, we were under Coach

Roland again. I'm unsure what happened, but Coach Roland said we wouldn't return to the Northwest Bulldogs. I didn't understand, but we were now playing for the Rosedale Cowboys. As a leader, this was painful because some of my teammates' parents did not allow them to come, and they stayed at Northwest. Splitting our team in half, breaking bonds, and destroying friendships.

At the beginning of the season, we picked up a new fullback from the Northwood Rams, the team now winning the National Championship two years in a row. Coach Roland gave him my position without even testing him or making him earn his spot on the team. I felt cheated. Worse, everything Coach Roland was trying to teach about fairness wasn't true. In hindsight, I know I should have gone to him and told him how I felt, but I didn't. Instead, my best friend Travis and I quit and went to play for the Liberty Lions.

We convinced our other best friend, Bryan, who played for Northwest to join us. Man, it was like falling from paradise to hell. The team was horrible. The parents were awful. The plays were terrible. I went from playing under the lights on turf to playing on dirt fields. In the very first game, we got our asses kicked. I don't remember the score, but it must have been close to a triple-digit loss. I tried to play quarterback, and Bryan and Travis were my running backs, but the rest of the team was so bad we couldn't get a single play off. I got sacked repeatedly, ultimately going home tired, sore, and humiliated.

Around midnight there's a knock on our door. It's Coach Roland. He sat me on our front porch, and Mama listened in the doorway.

"I saw your game today," he said.

"You guys looked like some shit."

I couldn't believe he'd been there. I was embarrassed. I wanted to prove him wrong, that I didn't need him or his team to win, but now I knew I did, and I hated that.

"Is this what you want for yourself?" he pressed.

"Is this who you are?"

I kept my head down. I didn't want to admit he was right.

"Look, it's simple. You can't quit my team. It's okay if your friends quit, but not you.

Why?" I asked

Coach Roland: *"Because you're not a quitter. Besides, you aren't even allowed to play for Liberty."* *"You signed an agreement to play with me."*

He pulled a piece of paper from his pocket and held it up and started reading it.

"This says you can only play for me on a team I'm coaching."

He let that sink in. In all actuality, I don't know what the paper said. I couldn't read so it could have said anything. Then he spoke to my grandma briefly, but I was so ashamed and absorbed by my thoughts that I didn't remember what he said.

"All right," he said as he walked off the porch.

Coach Roland: *"I'll see you tomorrow. Come to my house and get your shit, and don't be late."*

"Remember, if you do what I tell you to do and how I tell you to do it, you'll be fine."

After he left my grandma spoke from the doorway.

"You have to play for him, Al."

Then she turned and went to bed.

I sat on the step for a while by myself. I was still angry at Coach Roland for giving my spot away. If the boy worked for it or outplayed me, I would have been okay with that. I wasn't okay with him playing without earning it. Yet, I was relieved to be back on the team because I knew we would lose every game if I kept playing for the Liberty Lions. The following day, I went to his house, and he offered me my old Jersey, #40, I wore it to represent Mike Alstott, the NFL's top fullback. However, I wouldn't be playing fullback because the new kid from Northwood was given my spot. I needed a defensive number, so I picked #99 representing Warren Sapp, the NFL's best defensive tackle.

I accepted the change and was cool with the change. I was maturing and knew it was for the good of the team. Travis returned to play, too, and everything returned to normal. We went on to have a great year, we were a very talented team, even better than Coach Dj's team. You could go down the line, receivers, the Q.B., the linemen, they were all excellent. We had not one weak spot. We would win games by 30 or more points. I often had two to three sacks in a game. In one playoff game, I had eight sacks. My job was to keep the Q.B. on his back, staring up at the lights; it was a job I relished. However, Coach Roland was still hard on us, especially me. He sought perfection, and he came down hard on every little mistake.

In one game, we were winning 63-0; in the third quarter, Coach Roland put in the second team. When the other team scored, I knew we were in trouble; I could see it on his face. The final score was 63-6, but we had to run for an hour— laps in full gear after the game. That's how tough of a coach he was. We went to the city championship and destroyed Loch Raven. Then, we won the division championship against the Charm City Buccaneers, an excellent team. Next, we played an out-of-state team and humiliated them, winning 40-0. We were on fire, which left us one more game before going to Florida for the National Championship. We had a long bus ride to someplace deep in Pennsylvania.

I'll never forget it. The field was on a mountain. This was the first game where the officials would keep us from getting off the bus. We had to sit there until almost the beginning of the game. The whole thing gave me a bad vibe. For example, when I played for the Park Heights Spartans, they weighed me twice, hoping to disqualify me. When we got off the bus, they weighed me twice. The other team players were massive, with thick, hairy legs and some with facial hair.

The game starts, and the refs are calling all sorts of penalties on us, which never happened in the regular season or throughout our run for nationals. Coach Roland punished us so severely for the slightest infraction that we learned never to foul. We often went the whole game without a single penalty or very few, and now apparently on every other play, we are losing five or ten yards on penalties. At halftime, we were only down 0-13. We rallied in the second half and got two touchdowns to make it 12-13. Unfortunately, in the fourth quarter, they scored again, and we couldn't match. When the final whistle sounded, the other team celebrated. I still hear Queen - We Are The Champions playing in the background. *"We are the Champions."* It still makes me sick to listen to that song.

"We are the champions, my friends, and we'll keep fighting until the end. We are the champions. We are the champions. No time for losers 'cause we are the champions of the world."

Back then, it was the worst defeat of my life. Something inside of me died. We were at the end of junior high school, and our brotherhood and bond was over. We talked about winning a National Championship for Coach Roland as a team, and now that opportunity was gone. I stood on the field, tears running down my face; on the bus, all my teammates cried; I couldn't even look at Coach Roland. I felt I'd let him down. I sincerely felt I let my guy down, but it was a much stronger feeling than I ever felt for my father. Pretty soon, I had convinced myself that it was all my fault. We would have won had I only done a better job. That night, I didn't sleep. I kept thinking about it again and again. I remembered every play and what I should have done differently.

The following day, I called Coach Roland to apologize. His wife said he couldn't talk because he didn't feel well.

"Please," I said, *"it will only take a moment."*

"I'm sorry, Phonso, I can't let you talk to him…" There was a pause; I could tell she was conflicted by something and wasn't sure if she should tell the truth. *"It's…it's that he's crying."*

I was emotionally exhausted for weeks. I couldn't even think about football. There were no calls from any of my teammates, nor did I see Coach Roland. I was prepared to transition into high school. However, Coach Roland called me to say that a new unlimited football league for winter sports had begun. He wanted to know if I was interested.

"For sure, Coach."

In my mind, I said to myself, *"This is how I need to show my appreciation. Championship or nothing."*

"I mean, Yes, Sir."

It was a new league, and we would travel to all our games. There were no other local teams in Baltimore, meaning we would not be playing against our local rivals. There was so much unexpected pressure because I felt we needed to win for Coach Roland, and there was no other team to represent Baltimore. This would be my last opportunity to thank Coach for all he had done. Practices were brutal; we practiced in the snow since it was still winter. For hours, we would run play after play. For conditioning, we would run on slippery hills. After every play, snow was always stuck in your face mask, and your feet were always numb. Not one teammate complained; without saying anything, our mission was to bring a championship to Coach Roland.

The first preseason game was a jamboree; that's when you play many one-quarter matches against several teams. We played against the teams we would play during the season, provided no external teams existed. We took a beating. We didn't win a single game. Not making any excuses; they were stronger, bigger, faster, and more prepared than we were. It was a higher level of football than 11-14. Some of these kids had already had high school experience. Nobody said anything, but we knew. We knew it would be difficult to win a championship and to make matters worse; Coach Roland intensified the practices.

I admired my team because we were always responsive to adversity, mainly because it was second nature. To some extent, we were reacting to daily adversity. Many of us had to deal with traumas beyond our control, but we were unstoppable when we hit that football field. I don't remember how many games we played. Still, it didn't matter because we were undefeated and won the championship easily. This league was slightly different because the All-Star game was after the Championship Game. The collective of head coaches from the other teams selected the players for the All-Star Game. I was incredibly proud that other coaches saw something in me that Coach Roland saw. They also hosted the awards ceremony after the All-Star game, and a collective of coaches picked the Most Valuable Players. When I heard my name, it solidified that I did everything I could to bring Coach Roland a championship, but even more so, to put a smile back on his face. I won Team MVP with the Rosedale Cowboys, Team MVP, and All-Star MVP in the winter league that year.

The experience was great, but this was our last year together forever. I did everything to show Coach Roland that I respected and appreciated him for believing in me. It amazed me that I had been working so hard all these years. In my final year, I received recognition for my dedication and work. I wouldn't be who I am today without meeting Coach Roland, Coach DJ, Coach Barnes, and Coach Larry. The most memorable thing that Coach Roalnd gave me, which I still have today, is a plaque that reads:

Dear Alphonso Mayo #99

I started coaching football in 1998.

Since then, I've had a lot of good, talented teams.

With talented players, I've won a lot of games.

My 2002 team didn't possess the size or athletic players as the teams in the past.

On paper, you're known as The "Rosedale Cowboys."

But to the world, you are known as the Roland boys.

"The Best Team Ever."

Thank you for allowing me to help you be the best "us" we can be.

Love Always, Coach Roland.

The critical life lessons I took from Coach Roland, Coach DJ, Coach Barnes, and Coach Larry

- *Do it right-*

- *Do it to the best of your ability-*

- *Listen with a purpose-*

- *Never play favorites-*

- *Care for others-*

- *You'll only get what you have earned-*

- *Look a man in his eyes-*

- *Give Back-*

- *Great players inspire people around them-*

- *You Can't Quit-*

"Being perfect is about looking your friends in the eye and knowing that you didn't let them down because you told them the truth. And the truth is you did everything you could." - Coach Gary Gaines-

CHAPTER *12*
L.A. LESSONS

"You should never judge a book by its cover." - Unknown-

My second year on Violet Avenue, I met L.A. A few blocks from my house was an older lady who had a beautiful home with a picket fence and garden. She had this custom of giving away boxes of Tasty Cakes. Just like many of the neighborhood kids, she sucked me in. Every two weeks, she would open her door and give hundreds of boxes away to all the neighborhood kids. We loved that lady! For us, it was better than Halloween. One day, after I had picked up my Tasty Cakes and was heading home, I saw this guy on the street.

"Slick." He says,

"Hey, little man, make sure you have your parents check that."

He seemed concerned and sincere. He was dressed nicely. To my young eyes, he appeared to be wearing all-new clothes. He wore a nice watch, a gold ring, and Timberland boots. He had a caramel complexion and a full beard, well trimmed and tight to his face, with short hair.

"Check what?" I said.

"Your box of Tasty Cakes."

Me: *"Why?"*

"Is she family?"

Me: *"Naw."*

"Then take it home and let your family check it for you because you don't know her."

Me: *"All right."*

So when I got home, I did just that, and everything was okay. I didn't think much about our encounter but saw him a few days later while heading to football practice. We practiced at the PAL Recreation Center, and the field we practiced on was a few blocks behind the lovely lady's house just beyond Keyworth. I saw him on the way home. I suspected he might be involved in drug dealing, especially considering how nicely he dressed. It seemed like he was transitioning into a new territory, and his attire only added to my speculation. That was a dead giveaway. My initial observation while walking to school was that I knew that the Trinidadians were involved in drug dealings, operating from Springhill down to Keyworth Avenue, which intersected with Towanda Avenue. Meanwhile, the Black dealers focused on selling drugs from Springhill to Hillsdale. Here's this nice guy hanging around without a Trinidadian accent. While I haven't witnessed him directly involved in dealing, he's merely present in the area, perhaps keeping an eye on things.

One evening, my teammates and I walked up Towanda towards Hillsdale, where we all lived between Violet Avenue and Ulman Avenue. The streets were dark because the streetlights weren't working. The late fall season was taking its toll, causing daylight to dissipate earlier than usual. As we followed our routine of walking home together, we couldn't help but notice a man in a trenchcoat with a shotgun protruding from the bottom, making little effort to conceal it.

"Walk the other way," he said in a thick Trinidadian accent.

We didn't need to be told twice. No one said anything; we just turned up at Springhill to take Reisterstown Road home. After that night, I noticed more people getting killed in the neighborhood. It seemed like every few nights, there was a homicide—all between Keyworth and Springhill. At the same time, I started seeing L.A. more and more around my neighborhood. Every day, as I walked home from school, I saw him. He was always friendly. He would dap me up, meaning give me a high five. That made me feel cool, to say the least. He was so laid-back that it had a calming effect on me. I soon learned that he was running our neighborhood. He wasn't a dealer; he was a Kingpin.

It was perplexing to me. How could someone so caring be a Kingpin? Despite running a drug operation, he was openly concerned, even inquiring about the Tasty Cakes to ensure my parents checked them. It was just strange knowing he was not only involved but leading illegal activities while also looking out for my well-being.

When my friends and I would play crate ball (similar to basketball but with a milk crate attached to a wooden pole) on top of Violet, he would come over and play with us. He was always easy to talk to. He would ask how we were doing in school, about football, and ask about our families. He always looked out for us and wanted to ensure we were all right. L.A. never mentioned what he did. He started coming to the football games, too. He came to watch me every week for a while. I'd see him in the stands or on the sidelines. He was like a big brother; despite knowing what he did, I didn't care because he always showed love and support.

One day, L.A. and I were playing crate ball and having one of our routine talks, and the police came up and frisked him. It didn't phase him in the slightest. They asked him to remove his Timberlands. He said nothing as he obliged. He was utterly compliant but never said a word. While they checked his shoes, he kept dribbling and taking jump shots. So cool, unfazed, and calm. The cops found nothing and left. He looked at me and said, *"It's cool,"* and we continued playing.

Later that week, I saw him, and we went and played some crate ball together. When we finished, he said,

"I never want to see you out here."

I knew he meant hustling.

"Walk with me," he said.

We went about three blocks, and there were a bunch of guys sitting on a corner. They were drug dealers, young men in their late teens and up to their late 20's.

"Hey," he says, *"you see this kid? He can't hustle around here. If you see him out here, let me know. If I see him hustling with any of you, I'll kill you."*

Nobody said a word back to him, and we walked off. Initially, I thought it might be some recruitment tactic, but it turned out to be the opposite. There were plenty of other kids around, but he didn't make an effort to shield them from getting involved in the drug game. He specifically made it clear that I wasn't allowed to go down that path, and I didn't. Unfortunately, I couldn't say the same for all my friends.

I saw him a little less after our conversation and my encounter with the drug dealers. One day, when I was coming home from school, I walked from Springhill up through Towanda, similarly to how I walked from practice. I was with my friend Tellus, and once we got to his house, I said, *"Ard, I'll catch up later."* I saw L.A.'s Chevy Tahoe sitting by the alley. I saw him in the truck, windows down, and I was going to dap him up, but something was different. He wasn't as chill as every other time when he saw me. His calmness vanished, leaving behind a visage etched with rugged determination—a familiar sight from my childhood. His eyes, once warm and inviting, now veined with the shadows of violence, spoke volumes. He yelled.

"Go home now. Run!"

I didn't hesitate. I took off at a full sprint. It was maybe fifty yards to my house, and I was there in seconds. I made it inside, and as soon as my bookbag hit the floor, I heard gunshots. Like drums one after the other. *TAC. TAC... TAC... TAC.* Then I listened to the screech of tires and an engine revving and straining. When I looked out my window, the truck was gone. Later that night, I was in one of the front rooms of our house when I heard a woman calling. *"Help! Help! Help!"* I peeked through the blinds, and a car was rolling slowly down the street toward the woman screaming. Suddenly, a woman gets out and forces the other woman into the car, and it takes off.

That day was the last time I saw L.A. I didn't realize it then, but I missed his presence. I missed dapping him up and feeling cool when walking to and from practice. When I would go get the Tasty Cakes, no one was there to say, *"Have your parents check that."* I missed our crate ball talks. To give myself closure, I figured he was killed, which ended our friendship.

In 2009, I worked for Smart Steps Learning Center. A daycare and after-school program located across from the football field and recreation center on Towanda Avenue, where I played youth football. After several months of working there and getting to know my coworkers, I shared the story of a good man who was a Kingpin with Ms. Nancy. I explained that he never allowed or wanted me to sell drugs, and that possibly saved my life.

"What is his name?"

Me: *"I don't know his real name, but we called him L.A."*

With a big smile on her face, *"You mean Lamont. He's my ex-husband."*

She said he was always kindhearted despite living a not-so-pleasant lifestyle. She explained he was arrested and sentenced to 15 years. I listened to all the stories she could muster to tell. Ms. Nancy's stories painted a picture of a man with a generous spirit. She recounted how he bought food for those in need, paid strangers' electric bills, and even covered people's rent when they were struggling. When business was slow, he would have his hustlers mow yards, ensuring that their work benefited the community. Despite his actions, he never wanted children to witness drug dealing. It seemed that being a dealer was never his ambition, but circumstances had pushed him into that path as a means to make ends meet. She left me wondering how someone with such a big heart could be pulled into that lifestyle and, even more importantly, what made him see something in me and encourage me not to live that lifestyle.

It's never too late to save someone from what you should have been saved from. -Mayo-

CHAPTER *13*
THE BROTHERS I THOUGHT I HAD

"As we strolled home from practice one day, Travis, Bryan, Tellus, and I, a stranger approached us with a chilling prophecy. "One out of the four of you will make it," he declared, his words cutting through the air like a knife. "You have to decide who it will be." His grim forecast continued, painting a picture of our future: "More than likely, one of you will be shot and killed, one will be arrested, one will be strung out on drugs, and the other will do something positive." Man he was right.
-Mayo-

My friends and I would walk the streets and fuck people up. I feel bad about it now, but that's what we did. We didn't rob them; we just banked them. And we didn't mess with women or kids. It was about the fear we put in them. I guess it was about power also, because we lacked it in every sense growing up. It was fun, plus we had a strategy. Two or three of us would be on one side of the guy at a distance, then someone else, who appeared to be alone, would stroll up on the other side until the victim looked over at him. Then the rest of us would jump him.

This one time sticks out because it didn't work quite right. It was crazy. It was right after school, still light out. We were walking down Reisterstown Road. It was Bryan's turn to walk beside the victim, and Travis and I were set to bank him. But when Bryan stepped beside him, the guy was ready.

Guy: *"Hey, what are you doing?"*

Bryan: *"Uh, nothing."*

Guy: *"Are these your friends?"*

He knew we were together. *"Come over here!"* When we tried to walk away, he got angry. *"Where the fuck are you going? Sit down."* Suddenly the roles were reversed; it looked like he was going to beat us up. He was a fairly big guy too, black like us, in his mid-30's and in shape. He was no junkie. Bryan acted like he was going to sit but then bounced up and hit him. I was ready, too. I grabbed a loose brick and smashed it on the side of his head. That knocked him out cold. The guy was bald, so the knot rose immediately and started to bleed. Travis punched him in the face, and Bryan kicked him in the chest. I dropped the brick, and we took off running.

It was so easy for us to do things like that. There was no fear of jail or concern for who this person was. If he was someone's father or son. None of those thoughts existed in us, and we always did it. What we were doing to people, I knew we were destined to get caught or in trouble. Talk about being influenced by my friendships.

Football was my sanctuary, allowing me to escape my daily physical and mental reality. I spent hours away from home due to training and practice. I knew football could be my way to take my grandparents far from Baltimore. I was a leader on the football field and had brothers. I knew that whatever I did, my teammates and coaches were evaluating me, so I always strived to stay above and ahead of what was expected of me. It was good to have friends like Travis and Bryan because they made me better at football and fearless in the streets. They were my first best friends who I considered brothers.

In middle school, Travis, Bryan, and I decided to go into business. This was before my talks with L.A. Some kids set up lemonade stands on the corner, and we decided to sell drugs. We had one small problem, we didn't know what we were doing. In fact, we didn't even know what drugs looked like. We thought prescription drugs were drugs. So we stole a bunch of vitamins and over-the-counter meds out of our bathroom cabinets, ground up the contents, and put them in little baggies. We crossed the tracks (train tracks in another neighborhood) and picked some random street to *"sell drugs."* We never sold anything, but we would still talk tough. We'd call out, ***"Red tops, red tops!"*** We didn't know what it meant; we just repeated what we'd heard in our neighborhood. It's a miracle nobody shot us for moving in on their turf.

For months, we would front like we knew the street life, but we were athletes pretending. I was happy we were acting because I never wanted to sell drugs anyway. Then came the day Travis and Bryan were over at my house, and I was looking for something in my cousin Andre's closet. I don't even remember what, but I found a massive eight-ball (a fat bag of cocaine).

Travis and Bryan: *"Let me see. Let me see it."*

The boys were as curious as I was. Then I noticed a gun sitting there. It was a small one. I later learned it was a 22 beretta.

"Hey, check this out."

Once they saw it, they scattered. I'd never seen people move so fast, leaping down the steps four at a time. It must have been less than .000002 of a second before they were out of the house. I was left standing there alone. I shrugged. The gun was so small that I figured it couldn't do much, so I pulled the trigger. Nothing happened. It took me a while to convince them to return inside to see if the eight ball was real.

"My cousin Joe said that if it tastes nasty, then it's real," Bryan said.

Following this sound logic, we tasted it. It was nasty.

Bryan: *"What the fuck? It's nasty."*

Our tongues were numb, so we moved it into the room I shared with Mama.

A little later, my cousin Andre took me aside.

Andre: *"Yo, little Al, did you find something today?"*

Me: *"Whatcha' talking about?"*

Andre: *"You know what I'm talking about."*

Me: *"Yeah, I found some baby powder,"* I lied, *"because I needed it."*

He nodded slowly, trying to remain calm.

"Okay," he said, enunciating each syllable. *"What did you do with it?"*

"I put it in my shoes," I said.

Andre's eyes went wide. He raced up to my room. Lucky for me, we hadn't opened up the bag in a way to waste it because Andre would have indeed murdered me. I had to tell the guys the next day what had happened.

The simple truth is that not having a mother or a father isn't just a single blow to your life; it's an ongoing disability. All those things a good father or mother does were absent daily. Helping you get ready for school in the morning, supporting you when you are down, helping you with homework, and even kicking your ass when you deserve it. All those little things that a parent does every single day add up. And if you don't have it, it's like a sickness, like cancer, that keeps you from reaching your full potential.

For this reason, I clung to my friendships with Travis and Bryan. They were the closest things I had to real brothers. None of us had fathers in our lives, making our friendship even more important. I also benefited from having their mothers, especially Travis's mom, Ms. Niecey. She was a wonderful woman, short, stout, and strong. She had caramel skin, shoulder-length hair, and one gold cap on her left incisor. She was a force of nature. When she would come in from work, her presence would change the atmosphere. I felt Travis could do better because he had a mom like that. She worked at Fort Meade, and I remember she took me to work with her one day. She explained her job and roles as we walked around the base.

And I was so impressed.

She was a dedicated single mom raising Travis and his three sisters. She didn't play games and would whip them pretty often, sometimes in front of me. She'd use a belt, and if the message wasn't getting through, like my father she'd use her fists. That might sound abusive, but it never struck me that way. She was a strong mother. She took care of her responsibilities, and she was in charge. She became the example of what a mom should be, and I would sometimes wish that my mother would do for me everything that Travis's mom did for him.

The time I missed having a mom the most was during football season. When all the players' moms and some of the dads would be in the stands cheering and supporting them. After the games, the moms came and hugged and congratulated their sons. Not me, but at least I had Ms. Niecey. One memorable game was when we got so muddy that you couldn't even see the color of our jerseys. After playing in the State Regionals against the Buccaneers, we came out victorious. I recall her looking at us in the parking lot, shaking her head, and saying.

"Y'all aren't getting in my car like that. Ain't no way."

But then she smiled and gave us trash bags.

"Strip."

As we got older, Bryan started to change. He began obsessively talking about money and how badly he needed it. I wondered why, especially since his mother was actively involved in his life. The shift in his behavior puzzled me. I went to Bryan's house to find him one evening, but he wasn't there. I walked through the neighborhood and checked our usual hangout spots, searching for any sign of him. I couldn't find him anywhere. So, I decided to explore areas where we would never hang out. Despite the dangers in our neighborhood, there were certain blocks where we felt relatively safer.

Yet, there was one block we never ventured to—Hillsdale Avenue—the street known for being flooded with drug dealers. As I was passing through the alleyway nearing the block I heard his voice. When I looked up the street, I could see a smile on his face.

I said, *"What's going on? What are you doing?"*

His reply, *"Getting money, come on, it's easy. All we have to do is sell this weed."*

Since he was my friend and I wanted to protect him, I said, *"Okay."*

Pretending was one thing, but now it was a reality. Standing there with the drugs in my pocket, thoughts of L.A. flooded my mind—how drugs had plagued my family and wreaked havoc on my life. I couldn't escape the realization that drugs were the very reason I had been abandoned in that basement. I started walking and thinking about what I was about to do. I walked from Hillsdale Avenue to the 2500 block of North and Pennsylvania Avenue and back (approximately 4.5 miles). When I got back, I asked Bryan to talk.

Me: *"Yo, Come here for a second."*

"What's up, Mayo?"

Me: *"I can't do this. Come on, man, this isn't for us. We're football players. We don't have to do this."*

He looked at me and said,

"You don't, but I do."

At that moment, I realized I was losing my brother. It hurt, and I was at a loss for words. I stood there, reflecting on our younger days when we pretended to sell drugs, yet we never actually went through with it.

"Look, you know where I live if you need me," I whispered.

"I'm good," he said.

With one more attempt to save our friendship, I said,

"You know how this ends, jail or death; come on, man, don't do this."

With a stern voice, he said,

"I'm good."

As I walked away through the dimly lit alley, disappointment weighs heavy on my chest, accompanied by a profound sense of heartbreak. Each step feels heavier than the last, as if the weight of our shattered friendship is dragging me down. I deliberately avoid looking back, not wanting him to witness the pain etched on my face by his decision. It's as if our years of camaraderie, friendship, and brotherhood meant nothing. It was discarded like yesterday's news. His voice echoes in my mind,

"I got this one. I got this one."

His voice fading with each step. The next day, I went to Travis's house to tell him what had happened, but when I got there, his sister said he was with Bryan. Days passed without contact, then months and even years. I never lost my love for them. I never disclosed to their families the reason I stopped coming around. Periodically, I would stop by to check on them, driven by a deep-seated fear that they might end up incarcerated, harmed, or worse, killed.

What started as a double win for me became a double loss. I needed good friends, friends who could help me cope. Friends who understood what it felt like to grow up poor and broken. I needed brothers, but I also needed the benefits of their mothers. If life is a game, I'm 0-2 to drugs. First, it took my parents, and now it took the brothers I thought I had.

Chapter Thirteen Dedication

In 2012, during my sophomore year at Stevenson University, I received devastating news as I was training for football season. I was a mile and a half into my 3-mile run when I got the call that Travis had been shot and didn't make it. Later, I discovered that Travis collapsed less than two blocks from my house on Coldspring, and tragically, he was shot behind my house. In 2023, I learned that Bryan lost his life after a constant battle with drugs.

Travis and Bryan - your memories live on in the deepest depth of my heart. This chapter is a tribute to the indelible mark you left on my life and a testament to the enduring bonds of friendship that transcend time and space. You will always hold a special place in my soul.

Every negative is a positive. The bad things that happen to me, I somehow make them suitable. That means you can't do anything to hurt me. -50 cent-

CHAPTER *14*

YOU DON'T BELONG HERE

"Education is what remains after one has forgotten what one has learned in school."

- Albert Einstein -

It was only a few days into freshman year at Northwestern High, and I got into a fight. The day the suspension was lifted, I was called back into the principal's office.

Thinking, *"What did I do now?"*

Waiting for me were Assistant Principal Gray and a guidance counselor. When I walked in, he sternly stated, *"Have a seat."* I was nervous because I thought I was being kicked out of school. I had been in so many fights in middle school that I figured I'd reached the end of the line, and karma was catching up. What happened next was almost worse and certainly more embarrassing.

> *"Sadly, I must inform you that you're not in high school,"* Principal Gray said.

> *"Some mistakes were made, and you shouldn't be here."*

> *"You did not pass the Maryland School Assessment (MSA).*

> *I'm unsure how you got here, but you can't go any further in high school."*

> *"However, we can't send you back to middle school."*

He kept shaking his head, not quite believing the whole situation.

> *"We have a prep class you must pass before returning to normal classes. Do you understand?"* I didn't say anything. I was too embarrassed. My biggest weakness was on full display, and the fact that I still couldn't read was about to be openly exposed.

> *"Get your belongings. You're in 9-T."*

9-T was short for 9th grade transitional. It's similar to a remedial course that is offered in college. Remedial courses, or developmental or basic skills education, generally cover lower material and are aimed at students deemed unprepared for course-level work.

They took me to a closed room, and several other students were in the same predicament. That at least was a relief. The plan for the class was passed out. I figured I'd sit around, and this teacher would pass me like all the others did in middle school. I know, I know. It was the wrong attitude. However, the thing was, even though I had promised myself I wouldn't fight anymore, I figured I still didn't have to work in school.

The class was like solitary confinement. We stayed in the same room all day and couldn't even eat lunch with everyone else. It was a simple setup, too. Do the lesson plan on your desk and go home. No instruction or teaching. An introductory lesson plan. Next day the same process. At the end of the quarter, I was told that I had failed and would have to retake the class. I wasn't surprised, because I hadn't done the work. I figured no one else had either, and we'd all chill and wait it out until they passed us.

My thoughts, *"Fuck it."*

I returned to the same room on the first day of the second quarter. I'll never forget that moment. There's the same teacher, but no other students. I looked around, and there was just one lesson plan on the desk. I thought it was a prank for about an hour; then, I realized I was the only person who had failed. I was so embarrassed. In middle school, I had made fun of Special Ed. kids. Ironically, this wasn't even Special Ed; this was below that. My brain couldn't even process it. Then, I realized the only way to get out was to do the school work. For the first time, a school or a teacher wouldn't just pass me.

So I started looking at the packet, and I couldn't read it. I recognized a few words but only the most basic terms. It was like looking at ancient runes. I didn't want to quit, so I just stared at it. I could tell they were stories. You had to read stories and answer questions. It should have been easy, but I couldn't even read the questions. So I sat there all day with this one paragraph, trying to pronounce things, find words I knew, and guess the words around them. I spent all day on this paragraph. I took it home and kept looking at it. I still couldn't understand it, so I gave it to my younger cousin Solita. She read it effortlessly, as she said each word, I tried to remember it.

One word at a time. I knew the words verbally but didn't know what they looked like. Some words, like "ask," never looked right because I always said "ax." Then, I would take that same packet to my little cousins Davante and Deandre. They would read it, and I would try my best to memorize it. I spent a lot of time processing, making connections, remembering words, and reinforcing my learning.

Every day after that, I sat in that classroom and struggled. My mind started developing slowly, but my self-esteem was another story. Soon, I was thinking about language all day, every day. When someone would talk to me, I'd visualize how the words appeared on my work packets. Shortly after, I contemplated dropping out of high school because I felt embarrassed. Although I was making progress, I wasn't making it in a significant way. I was tired of going to school and going directly into that room. It was never unusual for me to go for a walk to process my thoughts. That started long ago when we first moved to Cherry Hill. I found myself walking down Park Heights Avenue aimlessly thinking.

"Man, I should just work."

"How are you going to play football?"

"You should get your GED."

"Do they have a football team at the GED school?"

"Just do it or have someone do the packet."

My thoughts were everywhere. I looked up, and I was outside a glass door. I couldn't tell you why, but I walked right into the Saint Ambrose Family Outreach Center. My mind was still racing.

"Go in," it said.

When I walked in, a Goddess greeted me. She was the prettiest lady I had ever seen.

"Hello, are you here for the tutoring position?"

Me: *"The tutoring position?"*

I didn't know what she was talking about. I had never heard about a tutor, nor could I spell tutoring. So I just agreed.

"Yes."

"My name is Ms. Tiffany, and you know we are paying youth to help our first and second graders with reading?"

Me: *"Y'all Pay?"*

Ms. Tiffany: *"Yes, $150 a month."*

In large part, I impersonated wanting to be a tutor because I wanted the money, but I couldn't read. Yet, that experience changed and saved my life.

I would arrive a few minutes after the first and second graders. The lead instructor was an Asian guy named Matt. This guy was a tutor expert extraordinaire, or at least I thought so. Students would come and have a seat. Matt would always say, *"Pull out your reading materials."* Like clockwork, I'd hear nothing but unzipped zippers and books flapping on the small desk. I would slowly pull up my seat and say, *"Are you ready?"* Like we were starting a race. All the students would yell, *"Yeah."* It was all about attitude. I'd start reading a line, and when I got stuck, I'd say something like *"You know what this word is, right?"*

And if they didn't know, I made them look it up in the dictionary. So I was able to learn it as well. It was a great experience learning from the first and second graders, pronouncing words, looking them up in the dictionary, and developing my reading skills—all while getting paid. Even though it was a struggle, I had to work a lot harder than the other kids because I didn't have the foundational knowledge and skills they did. I felt like I was ten years behind. Each time I would read, it took me hours and hours to complete simple assignments. For something big, like a paper, I would have to start three or four weeks ahead of the assignment. Matt was incredible, and he would help me from time to time. He would introduce me to new reading methods and books that I never actually got around to reading.

I worked this method the entire second quarter, and at the end of the quarter, I received my report card, and I couldn't believe what I saw. All B's and above! I was proud of myself for the first time in my academic life. I was good at football, but that was a given based on natural ability and practice. This was what I fought for. The feeling of getting out of 9-T was liberating and exuberant. Up until that point, I had never shown my grandma my report card. Throughout school, I would always trash my report cards. If Mama asked, I'd tell her I never got it; however, this time, I took it home. I had it in the front of my book bag. Nice, neat, and flat. Mama was cleaning as usual. I walked up all proud,

"Guess what?"

She said, **"What?"**

I said, **"BOOM."** And I handed it to her.

She looked at it. I saw her smile; she kept reading, her smile lasting longer, sticking to her face.

"Oh, My God."

She gave me a big hug. We were both so happy. Tears welled up in her eyes, and she began to cry. I realized I had achieved something truly exceptional. It was a positive outcome, starkly contrasting the usual emotions I evoked in her. This created a feedback loop, as for once, she experienced the sense of being a good parent—something she didn't get to feel too often. It filled me with pride to know that I could give her that sense of accomplishment, witnessing all her hard work culminate in something positive. At that moment, I consciously decided to provide her with that feeling as much as possible throughout the rest of her life.

By the beginning of my sophomore year, I was finally on track. Life wasn't easy, but I now had some tools and the work ethic to succeed. This was my moment to distinguish myself from the rest of my family, to prove I was different. I had finally found a way; succeeding in school, which gave me new confidence. I finally felt I deserved to be there. I was proud and had a lot of school pride. I was turning a corner, which was a combination of two things: wanting to make Mama proud and not wanting to feel shame.

I wanted to make her proud, channeling the same determination I had on the football field into achieving excellent grades whenever the opportunity presented itself. I loved that feeling because it reminded me of the feeling my Uncle George had given my grandparents. I noticed many of my classmates took their learning abilities for granted. Since I did not possess those same skills, I did not have time to mess around. I also worked hard to develop personal relationships with all my teachers. If I could show them my work ethic, they would be more willing to help me.

During this period, my cousin Nicole decided to get a tattoo, and, caught up in the enthusiasm of youth, I thought it would be cool to get one as well. I discovered the tattoo artist was a relative to her. Marcus, with his dark complexion, short stature, and low-cut hair, possessed a commanding presence. His broad nose and thin mustache framed his face. He shared a similar build to mine, being short and stocky. I immediately took a liking to him. He was down-to-earth and welcoming. He told me, *"Any family of Nicky's is family of mine."* We talked the entire time he was doing her tattoo.

"What are you into?" he asked.

"Football, school, video games," I said.

I told him I liked football. He said, *"Oh, I don't know anything about football."*

I gave him a sideways look; you live in an all-black community. I know he went to an all-black school. Why didn't he know anything about football? It was strange, but he was cool, so I let it go.

Marcus: *"What school do you go to?*

Me: *"Northwestern."*

Marcus: *"How are your grades?"*

"They are okay," I said.

Marcus: *"What's okay?"*

I told him I was returning to regular classes because I'd been in the 9-T, ninth-grade transition class. He nodded his head slowly, examining me.

"Tell you what, if you can bring me a report card with 80s or better, you'll get a tattoo on me."

I squinted in skepticism.

"Really?"

"Yeah," he said. *"Really."*

"I said, bet, you've got a deal."

I was skeptical because promises in my life had a history of being broken. However, I decided to put him to the test. I made a firm resolution that I could not and would not earn any grades below 80%. It was non-negotiable. With no money in hand and tattoos being costly, I dedicated myself to working exceptionally hard that quarter. Day and night, my focus was on earning a new tattoo. At the end of the quarter, and for the first time, I made the honor roll. That day, I walked to Marcus's house, just a few blocks from my grandmother's, and knocked on the door. He recognized me immediately.

"Hey, come on in, Al, you got something for me?"

I handed the report card over, and he said,

"All right, I got you; let me take care of these clients first. While you wait, you can take a look at these books. Pick anything you like."

I sat in his house until midnight but left with a new tattoo. It was my last name with my football number under it. I was so happy. I would hold up my end of the promise now that I knew this deal was real. I had found a new reason to take my education seriously.

The tattoos worked, but the most pivotal moment in high school for me was when I thought my Jewish teacher was being racist. Mr. Cohen approached my desk, looked me in the eyes, and said, *"Mayo, why don't you people study?"*

"You people," I said.

Instantly, my emotions heightened, feeling offended and ready for an argument;

"What do you mean, you people?"

Mr. Cohen quickly said, *"You and your friends."*

Then, he rephrased the question.

"Mayo, do you study?"

I thought, *"What did he say to me?"*

I responded *"Yes, when you ask us to or a teacher says we have a quiz or test."*

Mr. Cohen: *"So you only study when someone tells you what to do?"*

Me: *"Yes, I replied. Isn't that what you are supposed to do?"*

Mr. Cohen: *"No, it's not what you're supposed to do. You're supposed to study because you want to get better."*

Mr. Cohen: *"How often do your friends study?"*

Me: *"I don't know."*

Mr. Cohen: *"Well, Mayo, if that's the case, you'll only become as good as someone allows you to become."*

Mr. Cohen: *"How often do you play video games?"*

Me: *"I don't know, about 3 to 4 hours a night."*

Mr. Cohen: *"Okay, give me 15 to 20 minutes out of your evening. Play the game for three and a half hours and reserve the other 30 for studying."*

That's easy, I thought to myself.

Mr. Cohen: *"I guarantee you that if you study for about 15 to 30 minutes daily, you will outpace your peers because you're investing in yourself."*

I sat and listened, thinking what he said was ridiculous, but I decided to take him up on his offer. From that day, my study habits changed. I studied for his class for about fifteen to thirty minutes every evening. I thought nothing of it, but the information became easier to understand during his class. As he would lecture, answers and questions came to me effortlessly. As we prepared for our final exam, which had about a hundred questions, studying came naturally, and thirty minutes turned into an hour. On exam day, I felt prepared. I felt confident. I didn't think about it; I went through the questions swiftly. Fifteen minutes had passed, and Mr. Cohen noticed that my exam was complete and asked me to grade it on the spot.

"Yes, please."

Curious to know if my studying paid off.

Mr. Cohen: *"Wait in the hallway, and I'll call you back."*

Ten minutes later, Mr. Cohen asked me to come to his desk.

"You skipped two questions; why?"

He read the question and asked me to answer. After providing my response, he said,

"Correct. I'm incredibly proud of you. However, I cannot give you credit for the answers you missed. You would have gotten 100% if you didn't skip those two questions. Take your time, Mr. Mayo."

He dismissed me from the classroom, and as I turned to walk out, one of my teammates and good friends was taking his exam. He quietly whispered,

"Bro, wait for me in the hallway."

Me: *"Okay."*

Here I am, thinking it would be another five to ten minutes. Twenty minutes pass, then an hour. Completely frustrated, I looked into the classroom and said,

"Bro, what the hell are you doing?"

He looked at me and said,

"My exam."

Once he came out, I only had one question.

"Bro, did you study?"

Friend: *"Of course not."*

At that moment, I realized Mr. Cohen was correct. I had significantly separated myself from my friend by making a small investment of time in my studies. I studied 15 to 30 minutes daily for three months, between 900 and 1800 minutes more than my friend and teammate. I felt good, but at the same time, it was heartbreaking to know that this is how the world works and that most of my classmates, teammates, and family did not think like this.

Mr. Cohen taught me that if you are **persistent** and **consistent** and you willingly choose to invest in yourself, you will have a better chance at life. It wasn't like I was more intelligent than my teammate or that I somehow possessed some unique gifts that he didn't. The difference was that Mr. Cohen asked me a question that ignited a thought. He then provided a solution to help close the gap. I studied and was prepared, and my friend didn't and was unprepared.

Twenty-two tattoos later, I have Marcus to thank. His art became my way of self-expression, my grandma's smile became my why, and Mr. Cohen gave me the formula to be successful in life. I didn't do so bad for a kid that didn't belong in high school. I eventually graduated high school 9th overall with honors.

"Proper Preparation Prevents Poor Performance." *-James Baker-*

The world has permission to tell you where you don't belong, and you have permission not to believe it. -Mayo-

Gratitude Reflection:

My Childhood Guiding Spirits:

I would be remiss if I did not mention the most influential people from my young life. There would be no promise without them.

- Coach Roland Brown, my youth league football coach, taught me levels of discipline that I'm not even sure you can learn at a college level. He loved me and all my teammates. He was harsh but fair. He required greatness and displayed appreciation as he felt fit. I still strive to live up to the example he set for me alongside:

    » Coach DJ

    » Coach Ty Johnson

    » Coach Nathaniel Bond Sr.

    » Coach Larry

- Denise Braxton was like my mother. Her love for me was no less than any of her children. One day, she looked at me and said something that changed my life, ***"When are you going to be tired of embarrassing your family?"*** That sticks with me to this day.

- Ms. Jamie Rogers, my childhood nurse turned Godmother, played a pivotal role in my life. She not only cared for me but also took on the responsibility of raising me, providing unwavering love and a sense of security. When we first crossed paths, I was broken and navigating the lowest point in my life. However, Ms. Jamie consistently showed up, offering love and support that began the process of healing and rebuilding.

- Mr. Greg and Ms. Tiffany led the St. Ambrose Outreach Center youth program and gave me my first job as a tutor.

CHAPTER *15*

FINDING MOM

There's this iconic scene from The Fresh Prince of Bel-Air where Will asks Uncle Phill about his father, Lue. Will's father was absent but decided to plan a fishing trip with Will to reconnect and bond. Will is so excited and decides to get his father a gift, only to learn that Lue decided to stand him up and cancel the trip. Will pretends to be ok but has a breakdown. He looks at Uncle Phil and says those five powerful words.

"Why doesn't he want me?"

I remember the first time I watched it; it made me think of my mother and father but more deeply about my mother. I couldn't help but cry. Although it was a television show, the pain was real. When it came to finding my mother, it was like, Where's Waldo? It didn't make sense that she never came looking for or checked on me. I often asked, *"How can two people live in the same city minutes apart and never cross paths?"* I would frequently wonder what I did to her not to be wanted.

As I reminisced, a thought transported me back to a cherished memory from my childhood. I remembered being at Mr. Mike's shop with my father. On this particular day, I decided to make a quick stop at the store at the top of the block to grab a drink. As I approached, I could hear her voice, a distant yet unmistakable voice. It was the voice of a little girl, calling out my name from about a half a block away.

"Little Al. Little Al, I'm going to tell mommy I saw you."

I had never seen her before and only imagined her vicariously through my father's conversations. I thought to myself, *"This must be my sister."* Only my family and close friends call me Little Al. As she ran off, I followed her home, my gut filled with fear and apprehension.

"She has to live here."

I'm finally about to see my mother. Come here, little Al, the little girl says as she leads me into the vestibule of the rowhouse. I glimpsed inside to see a woman who was much more worn and spent than any vision of the mother I had created. The little girl yells.

"He's Here. He's Here."

The lady yells

"WHAT? Who's here?"

I stand patiently in the vestibule. Ten minutes becomes twenty, then thirty, and the little girl leaves with another lady.

"Bye, little Al."

More time passes. I could have waited for hours. I just wanted to see her. In my frail little voice

"Hello, are you coming out?"

She never answered. I peeked in again but didn't see anyone. She was leaving me no choice but to walk back to Mr. Mike's shop with the same feelings of emptiness.

After that moment, I gave up trying to connect. I had gone most of high school not thinking about her or her life. Not knowing if she was alive or well. Now nearing the end of high school, memories of when I was in seventh grade started to cloud my mind when I would ride the city bus and study all the women who looked about my mother's age.

On graduation day, as my classmates' mothers, fathers, and families cheered them on, I saw Mama's face in the back. True to her style, she always sat in the last row of the auditorium. Seeing her big, bright smile after every report card had become customary. As I walked on and across the stage nervously, I fixed my eyes on her. There she sat, radiating with pride. Our connection was truly special. I was extremely excited, happy, and proud of myself because it felt like I was doing something right. But in the back of my mind, for some strange reason, I wondered if my mother would be proud of me.

I was heading off to North Carolina Central University and decided to move early to live with my girlfriend the summer before the semester started. With little hope, I searched for my mother one last time. I found myself tracing the paths to the old addresses my father had once given me. I wandered to the house where I had spent hours waiting. Yet, with each visit, I was met with the stark reality of vacant and abandoned homes. I eventually asked my father if he had run into or seen her around.

"Little boy, no, I haven't seen your mother, nor do I desire to."

I spent weeks trying to figure out where she lived. A few weeks before heading to North Carolina, my father returned with some information after running into Tammy who I assumed was one of my aunts because of the name, but was my uncle on my mother's side.

"Little boy, she lives over there by Franklin Ave."

Without hesitation, I got a hack. I went to her location with a copy of my diploma and the biggest prom picture I could find. When I got there, the connection was faint. I didn't know what to call her. I didn't even know what to say. This would be a good start if I wanted to move forward with my life.

"Little Al, I apologize."

Me: *"I didn't come here for an apology."*

I didn't want it, nor did I need an apology. We talked for some time, and we even exchanged phone numbers. Weeks passed, and I didn't hear from her, so I decided to reach out to her, but when I did, her phone was disconnected. The day I left for North Carolina, I tried to call her one last time.

"The number you dialed is disconnected. You may want to check the number and dial again."

I boarded the Greyhound with the tickets that Coach Woodson had purchased for me. I figured the relationship I desired wouldn't happen. I thought to myself,

"You did your best."

I was moving hundreds of miles away, but my heart moved further from her. On my journey of discovering myself, I figured the best thing to do was move beyond the fantasies I held as a child. On that bus ride, I realized my mother didn't love me how I loved her, and I would have to accept it. A wise lady once said,

"Love is acceptance, Love is unconditional, Love has no expectations, Love is forgiving, Love involves devastation, and genuine Love is healing." -Jada P. Smith-

I only received devastation combined with fixation, which led to my humiliation. Even when I saw her in person, I never found my mom. I never found what I thought I was looking for. I never found what I believed I needed. God gave me the mom I needed in Gloria Mayo. I had neglected and verbally abused her. I didn't always respect her. That's when it all made sense.

You should have been there when I graduated

Told me you love me, and congratulations

Instead, you left us at the window, waiting

Where are you at mom? We're too young to understand; where are you at, huh?

Yeah, I know them drugs got you held captive

I can see it in your eyes; they got your mind captured

Some say it's fun to get the high, but I am not laughing

And what you don't realize and what you not grasping

That I was nothing but a kid who couldn't understand

I ain't gon' say that I forgive you 'cause it hasn't happened

I thought that maybe I feel better as time passes

If you really cared for me, then where you at then?

-NF-

Gratitude Reflection:

Northwestern Senior High Baltimore Maryland #WildcatPride:

- Mr. Guarino, my ninth-grade biology teacher, taught me to tie a tie.

- My ninth-grade math teacher, Mr. Harrison, who challenged me to be on time and take pride in how I look.

- Mr. Rapoport, the office administrator, allowed me to work under his guidance. This experience significantly boosted my inner confidence and self-esteem. Mr. Rapoport encouraged me to be a leader and inspired me to support and uplift my peers.

- Ms. Sheila Wright, my Early Childhood Education Teacher, welcomed me into a class predominantly attended by young women. Despite the gender dynamics, I gained valuable insights into early childhood development, including stages before the age of five. This experience also taught me the importance of collaborating with my female peers.

- My Early Child Care education classmates offered me an enriching experience that remains one of the highlights of my life. Beyond learning the art of nurturing children, I gained profound insights from my peers. They played a pivotal role in shaping me into the father I am today. While my initial motivation for joining the class was to engage with young ladies, the dynamics shifted, and these classmates transformed into supportive sisters. Their knowledge and encouragement motivated me to strive to be the best man and father possible.

- Mr. Cohen, imparted me with the invaluable lessons of consistency, persistence, and effective study habits. He emphasized the importance of dedicating 15 minutes daily to self-improvement.

Additionally, he introduced me to his grandmother, a Holocaust survivor. This encounter has left an indelible mark on my memory.

- Coach Carter, my lacrosse coach, believed in me and introduced me to the captivating world of lacrosse. Although I had other coaches in my life before you, you were my first official mentor through the school mentoring program. Your guidance expanded my vision for myself and improved my confidence. It could be the exhilarating match-up against Eric Pitts or simply your genuine love for the sport that ignited a fire within me. Either way, you played an instrumental role in shaping my journey; I am forever grateful for that.

- Coach Woodson, my football coach during my senior year, holds a special place in my heart. His belief in me as a player allowed me to push myself to new heights and leave everything I had on the field. He utilized my skills in multiple positions to benefit the team and embraced me as a son. He lifted me when I needed it the most. Coach Woodson was not just a coach to me but a pivotal figure in my life, a real model. I am forever grateful and deeply honored to have had the opportunity to play under his guidance. It takes a truly exceptional man to see the untapped potential in a 5-foot-6 player like myself and enabled me to excel as a Quarterback, Running back, Middle Linebacker, and Free Safety. Your belief in me fueled my determination. I want you to know that I gave every ounce of effort I had, both then and even to this day. The person I have become is a testament to your coaching, guidance, and belief in me. I carry your teachings and the values you instilled in me as a representation of the outstanding father figure you are. Thank you for everything, Coach.

- To my teammates, you were more than just fellow players - you were my brothers. I want you all to know I gave you everything

I had in every game and practice. Our win-to-loss record may not have reflected winners, but I knew and understood the battles you were fighting against off the field. And in my eyes, you were winners every day you showed up. Despite tempting offers from prestigious schools like Calvert Hall, Archbishop Curley, and the powerhouse Dunbar, turning my back on you was never an option. I would rather stay by your side, losing every game, than abandon you and have you fight alone. The bond we shared, the unity we had as a team, was far more important to me than any individual success. I want you all to understand that my commitment to you wasn't just about the game itself. It was about shared experiences, growth and resilience that we developed together. Despite the odds stacked against us, never doubt your impact on me. You taught me the true meaning of brotherhood, loyalty, and never giving up. I am forever grateful for the moments we shared on that field. I will always cherish the memories we created together. While I made significant contributions and earned the title of Most Valuable Player "MVP," my personal choice for the award would have been Lamback. He was a dedicated father and consistently demonstrated unwavering commitment by showing up every day and playing at his best. When I could not play in the final game, he donned the number 20 jersey. He delivered a remarkable performance that left a lasting impression. Thank you all for being there and fighting alongside me. #WildcatPride

CHAPTER *16*

COLLEGE INTERRUPTED

"When you go to college, focus on yourself and your sports. If you focus on the girls, you'll be home in less than six months like me." - Stefon, Steve Brother-

"Ma, we did it!"

"No baby, you did it!"

My grandmother never cared about receiving credit. Mama just wanted me to be the best I could be. She wanted me to be ambitious and follow my goals and dreams. Mama wasn't concerned about how I got there as long as I worked for it. Walking across that high school stage felt astronomically bigger than my circumstances. I knew that I had accomplished something to make my grandma proud, and according to the recommendations of my evaluation from Kennedy Krieger, I wasn't supposed to accomplish anything on my own. I was headed off to college in just a few weeks. For me, college was my way out.

I was the first person in my family to go to college, and I was filled with uncertainty. Questions flooded my mind, such as:

"How am I going to pay for college?"

"How am I going to get to North Carolina?"

"Do I have Financial aid?"

"Will I need a job?"

I received several scholarships to attend Towson University, a local school, earlier in the year. I knew that wasn't an option because I didn't want to stay home, nor did Towson produce National Championships or NFL-caliber players. So that was definitely out of the question. I received letters from Morgan State University on the east side of Baltimore, a bus ride away on Coldspring, which I knew wasn't an option either. I received interest from Columbia University, Syracuse, and Tennessee State

University; however, based on my motives, I was uninterested.

I had my focus set on North Carolina for one reason and one reason only, my girlfriend. My senior year consisted of me traveling back and forth to North Carolina to see her at her college. She attended Barton College in Wilson, North Carolina. Not only did dating a college girl give me somewhat of a status, but it made me feel good to know that I could see her occasionally and support her with the money I made working at Pizza Hut. It made me feel responsible and like a man. I would take time off of school to spend time with her. It was different from having a high school relationship mainly because it was long distance, and even though we grew up together, she seemed to be headed for bigger and better things than my female classmates.

Northwestern was no different than your typical high school. It was filled with drama, gossip, clicks, and frequent high school fights and breakups. But for the most part, I didn't have those problems because I was on the football team and my girlfriend was in college. Before she went to college, she attended one of Baltimore's top high schools. Baltimore City College High School, a well-recognized, respected, and known institution. She was smart, and before dating, we were neighborhood friends.

Before we became a couple, I endured the pain of my first relationship loss and heartbreak with my true high school sweetheart and love. High school relationships, especially in the 10th grade, can be tumultuous. We dated for a year, and in my youthful naivety, I believed we would be together forever. However, she broke my trust and heart by cheating on me. It was a devastating blow, one I struggled to recover from. Navigating my emotions was a challenging journey, because she was more than just a crush - she was the first young lady I truly loved.

As I struggled through my process of moving on, my cousin Solita started hanging out more with the young ladies in our neighborhood.

She would bring them to our house. It was in those moments that our conversations began. She started helping me navigate my feelings and broken heart. Then my homework. What started as a friendship transformed into something deeper.

Early childhood education was one of my favorite courses. Going into my senior year, I had been with my girlfriend for over a year and the same group of young ladies from my class for three years. We had a bond, and I genuinely trusted their intuition. We had frequent conversations about relationships and who we dated. They always seem to give sound advice. One evening, one of my classmates challenged my perspective.

Classmate: *"Mayo, you think she's faithful?"*

Me: *"Of course!"*

Classmate: *"Mayo, I'm telling you she's not."*

Me: *"What makes you think that?"*

Classmate: *"She's in college with grown men and has unlimited freedom. You're here in Baltimore."*

Me: *"I get that, but I go see her frequently."*

Classmate: *"Mayo, has she been to college parties?"*

Me: *"Yes, why?"*

Classmate: *"Even more reason. Freedom, parties, and grown men."*

My heart began to race, and I became a little irritated.

Classmate: *"Mayo, you think she loves you?"*

Me: *"Of course."*

Classmate: *"Well, if she does, when you get home, you should ask her if she's done anything with anyone else, and if she tells you the truth, she loves you."*

Me: *"Bet."*

I thought about our conversation for the duration of the school day. I was anxious about getting home and calling her to ask her. I didn't know how to ask but didn't want to seem insecure or like I didn't trust her. Neither was the case. For some odd reason, the day went extremely slow. I started to think about how I would respond depending on her answer. I got in around 7:00 p.m. that evening and called her on the house phone, our usual ritual.

"Hello."

Me: *"Hey, babe. How was your day?"*

"It was good; busy with classes and studying."

Me: *"That's good. Every day, you're one day closer."*

The small talk lasted another 10 minutes. I thought to myself, "How should I ask her?"

Me: *"Babe, today in school, we talked about college parties and girls. I have a question for you."*

"What's up?"

Me: *"Have you talked to anyone since you've been at Barton?"*

Immediately, there's no response—just an awkward pause.

Me: *"Hello, babe. Did you hear the question?"*

She burst out in tears. She explained how she almost hooked up with this one guy and that they had come close, but she didn't follow through. I was devastated. I was heartbroken. I started to think about all the times

I rejected a female classmate or easy sex. I thought to myself, *"**Nearly two years were wasted.**"* Even more importantly, I had shared with her my past trauma. I shared my fears of being abandoned, cheated on, and hurt. I trusted that she wouldn't do that. I became bitter, angry, hurt, and broken. I wanted to get her back. I wanted her to feel what I had felt.

The next day in class, the answer was in my body language. It further confirmed my classmate's intuition. Unlike most high schoolers, she offered empathy. She just said, *"**It will be Okay.**"* I became overwhelmed with my broken feelings. As a child, I never understood how to process my emotions. The only emotion I genuinely understood was anger. I wasn't equipped, and I became vengeful.

A month after graduating, I moved to North Carolina, and we rented a small apartment in Wilson. With little guidance, I didn't realize what I was doing with my life. Here I was, 18 years old, living on my own, six hours away from home, with a girl I no longer wanted to be with and who broke my heart. I've always been good at pretending and hiding my feelings. So that's what I did to push through. We were young and sexually active; that's how I coped with my brokenness. I pretended to be happy, but I knew that once I got to Central, I was going to attend the parties, I was going to flirt, and I wasn't just going to come close to doing something. It was going to happen.

Although getting revenge was at the top of my mind, I trained three to five days a week to prepare for college football. I was preparing to walk onto the football team in the fall but money was low and rent was due, so I had to find a part-time job. I eventually found a position about three miles away from where we lived, and because we couldn't always afford gas, I would jog to and from work to build up my endurance and cardio. It seemed fitting and helpful at the time. We always argued, so I found ways to tune her out. One afternoon, during an argument, I heard her loud and clear.

"I'M PREGNANT!"

School started in a few weeks.

Me: *"What did you say?"*

"I'M PREGNANT!"

"I'm keeping it this time."

Young, broke, and broken. I didn't say anything, but my mind wandered. She had gotten an abortion previously and didn't want to get another one. My mind was a whirlwind, thoughts scattering in every direction.

"What the hell am I going to do with the baby?"

"How am I going to raise a baby and play college ball?"

"How will I raise a baby when I don't want to be with this girl?"

Me: *"I'm heading out."*

"You should stay so we can figure this out as a family."

Me: *"Naw, I'm good. I'm staying on campus."*

"What am I going to do about the apartment?"

Me: *"You'll figure it out."*

I figured she would be ok because she had slightly more family support than I did. I can only imagine the emotional toll it took on her. I was immature and emotionless. I was selfish and cold.

A few weeks later I headed to campus. Back then, we didn't have GPS like we do now, so when driving to campus, I had to pay attention to the signs on the highway. I arrived on campus without money, family, or assistance. Need I say that I just left my pretend-to-be girlfriend back in

Wilson and her early stages of pregnancy. I didn't know what to do once on campus, so I just followed the largest group of people. I didn't even know where I was going to stay. I found myself going into the admissions office to gather information and being met with questions I didn't have the answer to.

Admission office: *"Did you take your placement test?"*

Me: *"What's that?"*

I had no clue how to navigate. I was directed to take my placement test, and I did. I left knowing that I needed remedial math and reading. They eventually went over my incomplete FAFSA forms. I had to register as an independent student. I also encountered a banker who introduced me to a credit card I had limited knowledge about. As the day went on, I received many phone calls from my girlfriend, but I didn't answer. I moved into my room, and I could only think, *"How the hell am I going to do this alone?"*

That entire semester I spent neglecting her and what she had going on. I didn't care to hear about her morning sickness, that her body was changing, and that she needed mental and spiritual support. I justified my actions with my thoughts.

"You cheated."

"You lied."

"You hurt me."

I spent the first few weeks of the semester in the gym, trying to impress some assistant coaches. Most of my time was spent running around the track to stay fit. Although I wanted to, I couldn't work myself up to talk to multiple young ladies. However, that semester, I did meet two amazing young women, but I wouldn't allow myself to get too close. I would openly share with my pretend girlfriend about the two young women to make her jealous, but no matter what I did, it never seemed like enough. She would pop up occasionally, but I would ignore her. Finally, at the end of the semester, she broke down because I offered little to no support, and she struggled to balance out her pregnancy and school work.

"I'm Going Back Home!"

Reality sunk in as I never wanted to be like my father. I knew it would be almost impossible to focus on college, sports, and girls and be a father to a child six hours away. So I decided I would go home too. That was the most conscious decision of all my choices until that point. At the end of the semester, I gave up all my belongings. Never to return.

I knew my future was back on campus, but my reality was in Baltimore—a place I never wanted to return to. I cried the entire ride home, knowing I was responsible for the outcomes. Not only that, I was extremely embarrassed because I was the first person in my family to go off to college, and I was the first person to return as a failure. I should have listened to Stefon. I left school to be the father I never had. I had to get a job, and I soon became very depressed. While I had a beautiful daughter, I was back in Baltimore, out of school, working for $7.50 an hour and off the football field. My relationship with my daughter's mother had already deteriorated, and then, perhaps most cruelly, my grandma was diagnosed with cancer and Alzheimer's.

"I don't know if young people know this, but the most important decision you will ever make after choosing to believe in God is the mate you decide to spend the rest of your life with. Your mate will either inspire you to grow into your greatness or will confine you to complacency. They'll even be your other half or make you half of yourself. Honorable Minister Louis Farrakhan said, "A good relationship will make you more youthful and bring out the best in you; a bad one will age you

prematurely and bring up the worst, so choose wisely."

-Nuri Muhammad-

CHAPTER 17

LOSSES COME IN TWOS

"Sometimes double or nothing can be a double win, but it also can be a double loss." -Mayo-

She didn't want to tell us, but we saw her body breaking down. We noticed her mobility decreasing. She used to always clean; now, she couldn't do more than a few minutes. She use to cook, but now she never cooks. She eventually got so tired that she couldn't even cash the family's government assistance checks. No one said much about her condition, but we all knew something was wrong.

"Ma, are you okay?"

"Yes, I'm just tired."

I would bring my beautiful baby girl to visit my grandmother, hoping to see her face light up with love and joy. I yearned for A'mia to experience the same warmth I felt as a child in my grandmother's presence. However, Mama would spend our visits mostly silent, sitting in her chair with a distant look in her eyes. I still felt grateful to be near her and cherished every moment we had together.

One evening, as I sat with Mama, I noticed a change in her demeanor. Her eyes bore into mine, and I could see the pain and fear in her face. Her voice was weak as she spoke, and I could sense the weight of her words before they even left her lips.

"Al, I'm sorry, but I have CANCER."

My heart felt like it had shattered. I tried to hold back the tears, but they came flooding out anyway. I really tried. I didn't want Mama to see me crying, but I couldn't help it. The thought of losing her felt like all the hurt I had experienced in my life all wrapped up together. I couldn't shake the feelings of hopelessness. At that moment, all the pain and trauma of my life felt like nothing. The woman who had been my rock, safe haven, and constant source of love and support was now facing the battle of her life. I knew nothing would ever be the same.

My cousin India and I became my grandmother's primary caregivers.

India did most of the work. We took her to appointments, ensured she ate and took her medication, and tried to keep her comfortable. The hardest part was dealing with the rest of our family. They were all so ungrateful and selfish. They expected Mama to cook and clean for them, even as she fought for her life. Seeing them take her for granted and treat her like shit was infuriating. Of course, none of them would get off their asses and help.

Uncle Riccas, in particular, was the worst. He was a mean drunk, and when he got drunk, he became a completely different person. He would lash out at anyone and everyone, including my grandmother. I would never want to leave my grandma alone because Riccas might start verbally abusing her. I could see the fear and hurt in her eyes as he hurled insults and cursed at her. It was like he wanted to break her, to make her feel as miserable as he did. The worst part was that he never remembered it the next day. He would wake up and act like nothing had happened, leaving us to deal with the aftermath of his cruel words.

I was filled with rage and frustration at my family's behavior.

"How could they treat Mama like this?"

"Didn't they understand how precious she was, how much we depended on her?"

I felt like I was carrying the world's weight on my shoulders, trying to protect my grandmother from the people who were supposed to love and care for her. At 20, the stress and anxiety started taking a toll on me. I couldn't say anything or complain about it because Mama needed me. One day, when I went to see Mama, Granddaddy informed me that she was rushed to the emergency room because she mistakenly pulled out her catheter bag. All he said was

"Al, blood was in her bag."

When I got to the emergency room, she was lying there with a blank look.

"Ma, I love you. Are you okay?"

She gripped my hand.

"Al, I knew you would find me. You always do. Where are we? Why are we in a truck?"

"We're not in a truck, Ma." I said, *"We're in a hospital,"* holding back my tears.

"We are, why?"

I tried to reassure her that everything would be okay, but deep down, I knew that it wouldn't and her condition was severe. The doctors told us that she had Alzheimer's, and they were doing everything they could to keep her stable.

"Al," she said, *"when are you returning to school?"*

School was the last thing on my mind. All the problems I had in my life seemed to over shadow any potential of returning to school. So I just said what she wanted to hear, *"Ma, I promise I'll go back and finish."* I was so afraid she would die that night, but she recovered. Her whole life, she had only been hospitalized once, so I was terrified. She had to stay in the hospital for a few days but recovered. Once my grandmother returned home, I figured my family would calm down and make things more comfortable for her, but I was wrong. As she lay on her deathbed, they continued to fight and fuss over the top of her. Many nights, she would wake up in a cold sweat, yelling. Mama slept in the dining room, I slept in the chair in the dining room and Granddaddy slept in the living room. When I would ask her if she was okay, she would reply,

"I was fighting with Al."

This means she had dreams of fighting my dad. Even though Uncle Riccas and my dad caused our family a lot of pain, my grandma had a soft spot for Uncle Riccas. For a short time her health started to improve, but then her health worsened and the house became unbearable. My cousin felt it was best that she move to an assisted living facility. I watched my grandmother's memory slowly disappear. Each day, she forgot more and more like our street address, her name, and even some of her closest relatives. Mama slipped further and further from reality and my reality began to deteriorate.

On the day the nursing home staff arrived to take my grandmother away, a mixture of sorrow, helplessness, and a sense of loss took over. I knew this would be the last time I would see her in our house, and that thought broke me. I watched her lying in bed, frail and fragile, and I took her hand in mine. I couldn't find the words to say, as everything I wanted to say stuck in my throat. All I could do was hold her hand, hoping she could feel the love I was trying to convey.

As I watched them prepare to transport her, my heart ached with the realization that I was saying goodbye to Mama. It felt like a blow to the heart. I wanted to hold onto her, to keep her close, but I knew deep down that it was time to let her go. I moved out of the way as they put her on the gurney. As the staff gently guided her away and towards the door I walked beside her. As she left, she kept saying,

"Riccas, come on."

"Riccas, come on."

"Riccas, come with me."

Uncle Riccas had gotten drunk that day, and he did the usual. He found an excuse to get angry and cuss people out. Both Aunt Berthena, Mama's sister who was visiting, and my cousin Pamela, Aunt Berthena's daughter, were victims of his words. In a fit of rage, he stormed into the basement.

"Mama, what are you talking about? Riccas can't go with you," I said, my voice shaking, but she didn't seem to hear me. Instead, she turned to me with a motherly look on her face.

"Al, when are you going back to school?" She asked.

As we moved towards the door, I tried to brush off her question because my heart was heavy with sadness. As they loaded her into the nursing home's transportation vehicle, I felt a part of me go with her. Mama was my source of comfort and stability, and now she was gone.

Everyone seemed depressed and sad. It was strange because our house was never that quiet. I watched silently as Granddaddy sat on the edge of his bed, tears streaming down his face. My heart ached for him. He just lost his best friend, his life partner, and the love of his life. A weird thought came over me, *"I hope my grandfather doesn't die from heartbreak."*

Her warm smile, gentle touch, and loving embrace made us all feel safe and secure despite our family circumstances. But now that she was gone, the house felt empty. The air felt heavy with grief and loss, and a deep sense of brokenness hung over us all. As I watched my grandfather struggle, I couldn't help but feel overwhelmed by my own emotions.

A few hours went by. Finally, my dad said,

"Where's Riccas?"

I didn't care as long as he wasn't bothering anyone. My cousin Mel went to the basement door and looked down.

"Riccas!"

"Riccas!"

"He's down here, at the bottom of the steps."

Mel walked down to the bottom of the steps to check on him.

"He ain't moving."

"He's just drunk," I said, *"Throw some water on his face."*

I got Mel a cup of water. I watched as he went back down and threw it on Uncle Ricca's face to wake him. Uncle Riccas didn't even flinch. That's when I knew something was wrong. Big Al and I went to the bottom of the steps to check on him. We could hear him breathing, but with short sharp breaths, like someone having an asthma attack. We'd seen him pass out thousands of times, but never like this. My dad yelled up the stairs,

"Call the ambulance!"

The EMT's rushed down the steps and put him on a stretcher. I remember they were swift, and the siren was so loud. My father, Pam, and India followed the ambulance. He was transported to the same hospital Mama was at just months earlier. I ran to the hospital. I kept thinking about what my grandma had said before she left;

"Come on, Riccas."

I got there 20 minutes after everyone else. India ran out of the room where Uncle Riccas laid. She was crying.

"Oh my God," she gasped. *"Oh, my God, he didn't make it."*

Two hours before, I wouldn't say I liked Uncle Ricca's. I was so mad at him for doing what he always did, getting drunk and yelling at everyone, but the hate turned into sorrow and I began to cry. I entered the room as he was lying on the bed. I held his hand. It was still warm.

"Sorry," I said.

Riccas passed on June, 9th 2008, he was 47 years old. His passing was a result of a fracture in his skull. The crack ran down the middle, causing severe brain damage and internal bleeding. I walked home from the hospital trying to process and digest what happened. When I got to the house, there were police, some in uniforms and some in suits. I was so drained by then, I walked right past them. I went into my room and cried. Despite Uncle Riccas saying many hurtful things, I knew he was fundamentally a good person. His alcoholism and drug addiction got the best of him, which means as a family we never did. His act of collecting cans, exchanging them for a small amount of money, and then giving it to Mama so our family could have something to eat was truly commendable. Similar to my father, he possessed untapped potential. I believe he could have excelled as a great electrician or electronic repairman.

Who was going to tell Mama?

My cousins and I planned to visit Mama at the nursing home a few days later. As we walked through the halls, those mixed feelings returned. The staff informed us that she had slipped into a coma. My heart dropped to the bottom of my stomach. I insisted that my cousins go in the room to see her first. I needed a moment alone with her, to soak in her presence. As I entered the room, it was surreal to see her lying there, so still and fragile. Her hair in cornrows, which was bizarre because she never did her hair like that.

As I got closer her breathing sounded similar to Uncle Ricca's when he was at the bottom of the steps. As I stood by her side, I knew it was inevitable. I leaned over, pressing a kiss to her forehead, and whispered, *"I love you,"* hoping somehow she could hear me. On the way home we all grappled with the impending loss. Instead of acknowledging it, my cousins shared their favorite stories about Mama, trying to hold onto her essence through memories. I remained silent.

Uncle Riccas's funeral was the next day, so we went to Reisterstown Plaza Mall to get some clothes. While everyone was waiting in line, India got a call. I didn't hear a word India said; but I could feel the despair based on the pitch and tone of her voice. It was a very familiar energy. I felt this before when my Uncle George passed away. I set the cufflinks on the counter and left the store. I wandered out of the plaza, down to Wabash Ave, and back towards Coldspring crying uncontrollably.

The one person that I thought I could never live without was gone. I walked past our house. I walked to Towanda Rec Center and sat on the football field bleachers, thinking about everything—my Uncle Riccas, Mama, and now my grandfather. How was he going to live? Sunset, and it got dark.

When I got back home, deja vu, reliving the episode from a week ago. Everyone in the house was crying, talking about Mama, saying they couldn't believe it, how they were going to miss her. I could have yelled as my thoughts were so loud.

" What the Fuck are you talking about?"

"You treated her like shit."

"You never cared about her."

Yet, I said nothing. I walked past them to my grandma's bedroom. I shut the door and sat on the edge of the bed. I must have cried all night. My grandma had a distinctive scent. I don't know what perfume she used, but it was in all her clothes. I've never encountered that particular scent on any other woman, not even to this day. I went into her closet and found one of her old blouses. I took it to the bed, held it close, inhaling her smell, and then I cried. I woke up the following day to attend Uncle Riccas's funeral.

No matter what happens or how bad it seems today, life continues, and it will be better tomorrow. -Maya Angelou-

Chapter Dedication: This chapter is dedicated to my grandmother and my Uncle Riccas. Despite the difficulty I faced in writing this chapter, I knew its importance. My grandmother passed away on June 16th, 2008, at the age of 77. Matthew 18:21-22. As much as I despised my uncle, I found forgiveness the day he passed away. Strangely enough, her connection with him was far stronger than with all of her other children, and when we lost him, we lost her too.

CHAPTER *18*

THE PROMISE

"With every loss, something great is birthed." -Mayo-

"Al, when are you going to go back to school?"-Mama-

Before she passed, I would listen to the song; Love Brings Change by Jamie Foxx.

"Maybe the world doesn't see you, and maybe they don't understand. Just cause you don't see the footprints don't mean that they're not in the sand. I know you're surrounded by strangers and feels so alone in your heart. But when everyone stands in the darkness, no one can tell them apart. Everyone has their own stories, and nobody's ends quite the same. I look for the days in the sunshine over the nights in the rain. But love brings change."

I would listen to that song again and again. It fit my feelings and everything that I was going through perfectly. *"Now all I want to do is see you laugh again and see that same joy in your eyes. I know that you tried, and you just keep on smiling, and everything passes with time."* I cried for hours and hours. I imagined her in heaven with my Uncle George. This was the first time in my life I understood depression. I had felt it before and heard how many people suffered from it, but I never experienced it to this degree. I stopped eating. I didn't care what day it was or what time it was. The only thing that made me happy was being with my daughters, and even that seemed a labor most days. I would walk the streets of Park Heights at 3 and 4 in the morning. At that time, it was considered one of Baltimore's most dangerous neighborhoods. I didn't care. Suppose someone had shot or hurt me; they would have been doing me a favor.

On the day of her funeral, all I could do was sit there. I wanted to share the song in my heart, but I didn't have the strength. I promised Mama I would be the first to finish college, but now she'll never get to see me do it. I felt I had betrayed her. At the funeral, I watched my cousin India pull her veil down before they closed the casket. That chapter of my life was over. I'm proud that every day for two years, I was there for her and told her I loved her.

Over the following months, I witnessed our family gradually separate. Our extended family, family friends, and people in the neighborhood stopped coming by. There was always so little love in my family, but this was different.

I would come downstairs in the morning, and Granddaddy looked sad and lonely. The man was heartbroken. Over forty years they had been together. Looking at him made me more depressed. I hated seeing him like that. My grandfather was always present growing up, but we had a distant relationship. Granddaddy was always around but never spoke much or expressed his emotions or feelings. He was a quiet observer, and his words were always humble. When my grandmother died, everything changed. We both needed each other to emotionally get beyond our shared experience of losing someone we loved so deeply.

It was as if we had been given permission to connect on a deeper level. Slowly but surely, we started to have conversations. Everything had been superficial before, but now we talked for real. We shared our memories of my grandmother and spoke about our own experiences dealing with her loss. Hell, I even sat with him and listened to Louis Farrakhan. I still didn't understand his teachings, but I did it to be with my granddad. I began to learn more about my grandfather's life, and I was proud to learn our family history. I started appreciating his presence in my life. He became a source of support and love.

I did my best to do whatever he asked because I knew he needed it, but so did I. He knew I was hurting financially, and he'd try to help me out. He would give me a hundred dollars to go to the store and buy something that cost only a few dollars, then tell me to keep the change. I never shared with Granddaddy what I was going through outside of our relationship. I never told him how difficult life had become, how much I was hurting, and how disappointed I was with myself because I believed he had it worse than I did. My grandfather was legally blind, but he saw through me. He knew that I was pretending. He knew I was hurting and our pain drew us closer together.

Six months later, my grandfather decided to get laser surgery on his eyes to remove the cataract. Since I was little, my grandfather's eyes looked covered by a glossy gray bluest base. My grandmother had tried to convince him for years, but he always made false promises. I guess he wanted to keep his promise to her because he somehow found the courage. After his surgery, he needed assistance. My cousin India and I provided care for about two weeks. One afternoon I walked into the house and he stood at the bottom of the stairs.

"Hey, Granddaddy. Why are you on the steps?"

"Waiting on you, Al."

"What's going on?"

"Nothing. I wanted to tell you that you are as ugly as you sound."

We both busted out in laughter. This was the first time my grandfather saw me. We hugged. Life had finally started to feel somewhat normal. I worked two minimum-wage jobs, completed trade school, and was finally on a better path. Yet, much didn't change with my family.

Then life threw me a curveball when I received a call from my cousin India, explaining that Grandaddy had suffered from a stroke. My heart sank. I could feel the panic set in as I tried to process the news. I didn't know how serious it was, but I knew it couldn't be good. Days passed and my grandfather remained hospitalized. I wanted to do something, anything, to make things better, but there was nothing I could do. All I could do was wait and hope for the best.

Unfortunately, the best never came. Shortly after, my grandfather was diagnosed with lung cancer. The doctors recommended that my grandfather be put in a nursing home, and my emotions reached a boiling point. I was angry and sad. I realized my grandfather needed more help than we could give him.

"God, what the hell. He's all I have left. Don't you know how much he means to me?"

The thought of my grandfather living in a nursing home, alone and helpless, was messed up. It felt like God somehow took something from me every time something was going right. It felt like God betrayed me. Like God was giving up on me. Like God was doing the very thing my parents did to me. Like God was abandoning me.

It wasn't easy to come to terms with this, but I figured my grandfather wouldn't make it. I went to see my grandfather bi-weekly, and even though it was painful to see him in such a vulnerable state, I was grateful that he was still with me. On March 10th, 2010, I went to visit him. He couldn't speak, but his spirit conveyed a message of hopelessness and fear. He started to cry. Remember he had only cried twice before. My Uncle George's and my grandma's passing. I looked him in the eyes and said,

"I promise, I'm going to make y'all proud."

The next day, I contacted my high school football coach and told him I wanted to return to school but had no support. I had not talked to Coach Woodson for years, and I spent most of my time back home avoiding him because I knew he was disappointed in me. I had heard from some of my old teammates that he used me as an example of what not to become. But I was desperate. I didn't have anyone. I visited the high school several times, hoping he would help me. He eventually agreed, and we looked at a few schools. He contacted some of his old contacts, but nothing happened. He called the coach of McDaniel College.

Coach Woodson: *"Hey Coach, how have you been? Look, I have a great young man here looking to return to school; you all got some space?"*

McDaniel Coach: *"Tell me about him?"*

Coach Woodson: *"He graduated in 2006; he was our best player. Came home to take care of his grandmother...."*

The Coach interrupted him.

"I'm sorry, coach, we're not interested. He's too old."

Coach Woodson: *"I understand, coach."*

"Look, there is a University in Owings Mills, and they are starting a football team. He should check them out. It's called Stevenson University. Good luck, coach."

I had never heard about Stevenson University. I applied from a Blackberry phone because I didn't have a computer. Well, it was a Blueberry cell phone, a knockoff of a Blackberry. Then, I called the university to see if they received my application, praying they would accept me. I kept reminding myself of my promise to return to school. I knew it was crucial for me.

Some time had passed and I hadn't been accepted. I kept seeing commercials from Stevenson University where the tagline was simple yet powerful, *"Reimagining your future."*

I called the university and they scheduled an intake meeting. This was my final opportunity to gain admission. Despite these hurdles, I was determined to prove myself. During my intake meeting I spoke to Ms. Candace Parker. I poured my heart out to Ms. Parker, telling her about my upbringing and how I had never been a great student until high school. Sharing about my intellectual disability and how that posed a challenge.

I expressed to her the significance of this opportunity and my commitment to making it a reality. I assured her that my grade point average would improve every semester and I promised her that if accepted my final semester would be a 4.0. I shared with her my promise to my grandmother, who had always believed in me, and my determination to make her proud. I knew I had what it took to succeed. I just needed someone to give me a chance.

"When faith and fear meet, it's called the crossroads of courage."-
Mayo-

Ms. Parker listened patiently as I spoke, and I could see the empathy in her eyes. She understood what it was like to struggle, to fight for your dreams, and then, she smiled.

"Okay," she said. "I'll get back to you."

Over the next few weeks, I waited to hear from her. I kept looking at my phone daily, but she never called. She never emailed me. On April 15, 2010, I received a call from Coach Hottel with excitement in his voice.

"Mr. Alphonso Mayo, this is Coach Hottel from Stevenson University, and I wanted to welcome you to Stevenson as a Mustang."

He said some other stuff, but I couldn't tell you what it was. Tears streamed down my face as I hung up the phone. I couldn't believe it. I had been accepted into Stevenson University.

After years of struggling and feeling like I would never amount to anything, I felt relief, gratitude, and, above all, joy. It was like a weight had been lifted off my shoulders, and I could finally breathe again. I could not wait to visit Granddaddy to share the good news. On April 19th, a few days later I walked into his room.

"Granddaddy, I finally have a chance to prove myself."

"I have an opportunity to fulfill the promise."

He couldn't talk because of his condition. But in his spirit, I knew he was proud of me. On May 22, 2010 Granddaddy passed away, and the only thing I had left was *"The Promise"* that I made.

"Some promises are meant to be broken, and some are meant to die for." -Mayo-

CHAPTER *19*

AN IMPOSSIBLE DREAM

"When the people in your life can't provide what you need in the most unexpected ways God will send you the people you need." -Mayo-

Over the next four years, my life became a constant cycle of working harder than ever. I was determined to keep that promise, but it wasn't easy. Attending a predominantly white school like Stevenson University was a culture shock. The academic expectations were high, and it didn't matter if you were a star athlete or a commuter student; you had to perform. I knew it would be a struggle, but it was all I had. Despite my best efforts, setbacks and challenges followed me everywhere. I poured myself into my studies, working long hours and overnight. Sacrificing sleep and social events just to keep up with my coursework. My personal life was falling apart. I struggled to make ends meet. I was juggling multiple jobs and responsibilities. The more I excelled in college, the more my personal life took a hit. We received a late notice for rent every other month.

My girlfriend didn't understand, and I didn't expect her to. She didn't lose her grandparents. She did know the last words Mama said to me were, **"Al when are you going to go back to school."** I knew I had to work harder than anyone else to finish. I arrived at the university by 4:30 am and left around 7 pm. It was long hours, but I had grown accustomed to it. My sacrifices, the hours spent in the gym, missing family events, and missing time with my children all seemed worth it. Driving back to my townhouse, I would see the familiar sights of Park Heights, the boarded-up homes, liquor stores, the trash on the streets, and the familiar faces standing on the connors. A reminder of the struggles and hardships that I come from and hoped to one day overcome. As I entered my house, I felt a sense of gratitude. No matter what was happening, I knew I had a purpose and was meant for something bigger than myself, and I was willing to do whatever it took to make that happen.

During my first year, Tim Campbell Jr., one of my teammates, asked me why I was so dedicated.

Tim: *"Bro, why are you always here?"*

"What do you mean?"

Tim: *"Bro. You have a family, work, children, and school yet you are always here first at practice. I see you leaving campus around 8 pm. Why?"*

"Bro, this is my safe space. It's the only time things feel normal in my life. I don't have much outside of this."

Tim: *"I respect you, bro."*

Tim didn't know I was struggling academically, personally, and barely holding on to my dreams. A year later, I met Ms. Christine Flex. I remember walking into the academic center feeling lost. I needed help with my studies, but none of the younger tutors assisted me in the way that I needed. That's when I met her.

"Hey, I need to talk to someone about getting a professor as a tutor."

The student worker looked at me like I was crazy.

Student: *"We don't do that. It has to be a work-study student."*

"I mean this in the most positive way. I don't need a student. I need an adult who can help me figure out this work."

I overlooked her standing at the desk, shaking her head, looking at what was happening.

Ms. Flex: *"How can I help you?"*

"I had requested to speak to someone higher up who could give me the professional help I needed to succeed at the university. I need an adult as a tutor, not a student."

Ms. Flex: *"I'll take it from here."*

She became my tutor from that day forward and my mentor. I didn't know it during our first encounter, but she was the President of the Academic Link.

Ms. Flex: *"Here's when we can meet. Be on time."*

"Yes, ma'am."

The first paper I gave her to review was marked with so much red ink you would have thought I wrote my assignment on red paper. I was embarrassed, but also grateful. She was honest and tough, but she wanted to see me excel. She would say things like:

"You can do this if you want to."

"Did you read over it before bringing it in?"

"Are you working hard, or do you want me to work hard for you?"

"It's ask, not ax."

Slowly, the red marks started to decrease. At one meeting, she requested that I say what I was trying to write.

Ms. Flex: *"Don't read; just talk to me."*

It was easy. It was natural.

Ms. Flex: *"Wow, Mayo, you are a phenomenal speaker. If only your paper could reflect your words."*

She motivated me, and I loved working with her. Together, we spent many hours in the academic link, working on my studies and building a friendship. I was honored when she asked me to speak about renaming the academic link. It was an amazing opportunity to represent the center, but more importantly, it was a chance to represent her. I'll never forget the impact she had on my life. She believed in me. She pushed me to improve, work harder, and achieve my goals, and I was doing just that.

A few weeks before the end of my sophomore year, I received a bill from the university for over **$10,000** - a sum I knew I could never afford. I felt like things were slipping away. I prepared to say goodbye to my dreams of graduating. I went to her and broke the news.

"Hey, Ms. Flex, do you have time to talk?"

Ms. Flex: *"Sure."*

"I'm sorry to tell you this, but I won't be attending Stevenson next semester."

Ms. Flex: *"What? Why?"*

"I can't afford it. I just got a $10,000 bill. I just wanted to say thanks for everything."

Not only did I have a big bill at school, but I was being evicted. She was upset, of course. But more than that, she was disappointed. I could see it in her eyes. And that pain cut deeper than anything. It felt like I was failing her, failing myself, and failing my grandmother.

Ms. Flex: *"You're not going anywhere."*

"I don't want to, but I can't afford to stay."

Ms. Flex: *"We will have to figure something out."*

I was still determining what my next steps should be so I did what I thought was reasonable. I emailed everyone in the President's office at the university.

"Dear President Manning and Presidential Council,

I hope this email finds you well. My name is Alphonso Mayo, and I am a sophomore majoring in Human Services at Stevenson University. Additionally, I am a dedicated member of the football team.

I am reaching out to you today with a heavy heart as I am faced with the unfortunate situation of potentially leaving the university due to financial constraints. While you may not know me personally, I have overcome numerous obstacles and challenges to be part of this esteemed institution. I have diligently strived to contribute positively to the university community in various ways.

I have actively engaged in community service projects, including those with Habitat for Humanity. Furthermore, I have attended every class without a single absence and poured my all into both football practice and being a valuable member of the team. Despite my best efforts, I cannot afford the costs of continuing my education here at the university.

Recently, I was notified of a bill that I cannot cover. I am doing my best to navigate this financial challenge while balancing my personal life. As the father of four beautiful children, I work several part-time jobs to provide for them, in addition to my commitments to the Stevenson University community.

This represents my second chance at life, unlike many of my peers and colleagues. I promised my grandmother that I would be the first person in my family to graduate from college, and this is my only opportunity to fulfill that promise. I am reaching out in the hope that you might provide support or guidance.

I understand you have numerous responsibilities, and I am unsure of the appropriate channels to address this issue. If you could kindly direct me to the right person or department, I will do my utmost to fulfill my part of any necessary arrangements.

Thank you very much for your time, consideration, and the invaluable support you provide to our university community.

To my surprise, the next day, I received a response from Mr. Tim Campbell, the university CFO. In his email, Mr. Campbell instructed me to go to the financial aid office to visit Sarah Mansfield. He didn't elaborate on why but clarified that I needed to do so. When I arrived at the financial aid office, I asked for Ms. Sarah Mansfield. She greeted me with a warm smile and invited me to have a seat. She then explained that Mr. Campbell had spoken to her about my situation.

"Thank you for coming by, Alphonso."

I sat in my seat, a bit nervous.

"Hello."

Ms. Mansfield: *"We received instruction from Mr. Campbell. Your bill has been cleared, and you'll receive aid to cover the rest of your education at the university. You'll also receive student-work study and need to meet with Morgan Somerville."*

I didn't know Mr. Tim well, nor had I spoken to him prior, but because of him, I could continue college and pursue my dreams. Talk about divine intervention. I had never met Mr. Campbell before, but I put two and two together and realized that he might be the father of my teammate Tim.

I reached out to Tim, who confirmed that his father did indeed work at the university. I didn't tell him the full extent of my situation, but I told him I was extremely grateful for his father's work. I was overcome with gratitude. Tim was one of the first teammates who recognized that I was working so hard and to think about his father helping me; I was overwhelmed with emotion and couldn't thank him enough. I am forever grateful for his help and will never forget his impact on my life. When I reminisce on my college years, I am thankful for the many individuals who supported me. They didn't have to help me, but they did, and by doing so, they showed me the meaning of kindness and compassion.

Many people played a significant role in my success. Mr. Rick was more than just a supervisor; he was a father figure and a mentor. He believed in me while employing me. Then there was Morgan; she helped me secure a work-study position, which not only assisted me financially but also allowed me to build meaningful relationships with other students on campus. She became a dear friend, always there to lend an ear or offer a word of encouragement. Mr. Mitch was not just a supervisor but also a friend and mentor to me. He always had a positive attitude and a great sense of humor, which made our work environment enjoyable. He made everyone feel appreciated and valued, which motivated me to work harder and do my best. Rhonda Arnold epitomized the essence of a big sister in times of need. Countless on-campus tickets never made it through the system. She became the grace I needed to fulfill the promise. Rhonda's presence was a constant source of support, always welcoming, loving, and greeting me with a smile.

These people played a huge role in my life and helped me through a difficult time. Their kindness and generosity have stayed with me, and I strive to pay it forward by helping others. I am grateful for the lessons they taught me and their impact on my life. They will always hold a special place in my heart.

My college experience was a lot like my police experience. In one instance, I was on the verge of dropping out of school because of financial issues. It was a bitter pill to swallow. The thought of my dreams being shattered because I couldn't afford to pay the tuition fees. However, the glimmer of hope in getting the financial support I needed and having a supportive community of people who believed in me changed my outcome. They reminded me that I could be and do anything I wanted to be and achieve anything I set my mind to. With their support, I found a way to make it work. I was working three jobs on campus. Looking back, it wasn't easy; I realize that my college experience tested my resilience and determination, something my entire life was preparing me for.

"Not everything that is faced can be changed, but nothing can be changed until it is faced." -James Baldwin-

CHAPTER *20*

GRADUATION

"We must accept finite disappointment, but never lose infinite hope."-MLK-

Finally, the day my grandmother had dreamed about, and I had been working for, had arrived. Graduation. **FINISH!** Although it wasn't for me, I was proud to be the first person in my family to graduate college. I pushed and fought through every essay, quiz, and final exam. I survived countless grueling football practices and games. I persevered through everything outside the university and I'm now ready to walk across the stage.

As we arrived on campus, I walked over to get the additional tickets for my family. We were greeted by one of the campus staff. I asked if they could escort my family into the gymnasium for the ceremony. I walked outside over to the campus entrance to take a deep breath. I looked at the small practice field we used during my first year of football and the Human Service building where most of my classes were held. I walked down to the fitness gym that was always empty, remembering that's where I found peace most days. As I walked back, campus staff stopped me.

"Alphonso, President Manning, and Tim Campbell would like to speak with you in the guest room."

There was a sense of anticipation as I entered the room. I wasn't sure what to expect, but I knew the conversations in that room would be filled with gratitude and congratulations. I couldn't help but feel a sense of accomplishment. I saw all the provost, special guests, speakers, commencement speakers, and executives in one place. Thinking to myself,

"I don't see any other students."

As I approached the back of the room, I couldn't help but feel a sense of awe at the magnitude of this moment. This was the culmination of years of hard work. Mr. Tim greeted me first,

Mr. Tim: *"Alphonso, it's great to see you. We have someone we would like to introduce you too."*

Mr. Tim: *"Alphonso, meet Mr. Byron Pitts, ABC News Anchor, and our Keynote speaker."*

Mr. Pitts: *"Alphonso, it's a pleasure to meet you."*

"You as well, Sir."

Mr. Pitts pulled me aside and we had a brief conversation as the ceremony was about to start. He informed me that the university president had mentioned me several times and that he was incredibly proud of my accomplishments and fight. I felt tears welling up in my eyes as he spoke, overwhelmed by the knowledge that I had made such an impact. He briefly shared his upbringing in Baltimore and how he had struggled to reach the level of success he did. He shared his struggles with literacy and his inability to read growing up. His words were filled with empathy and understanding, and I felt a sense of connection with him.

As they started to call the guests into the gymnasium, he looked at me again and said, *"You did it, and you should be proud."*

I felt a gentle hand on my shoulder as we returned to the front. I turned to see Mr. Tim standing beside me with a warm smile.

"Alphonso, one day, I am going to work for you."

That was a high honor. It was a surreal feeling I knew I would hold onto for the rest of my life. It should be a momentous occasion as I took my seat, but I couldn't help but feel a sense of loneliness. As I gazed out at the crowd, seeing so many families beaming with joy, pride, and taking pictures, I felt a gaping void in my heart as I thought of the absence of all the people who should be here but aren't. My mother, father, Uncle George, Uncle Riccas, Granddaddy, and most painfully, Mama.

Yes, I had made it, but it seemed so much more costly than everyone around me could understand. In many ways, I felt like the scared, unimportant, and insignificant child I once was. Nevertheless, I tried my hardest to push these thoughts aside. I gaze over at my family; I look at my son and daughters and force a smile, while inside, my heart is heavy with grief. As I sat in my seat, surrounded by fellow graduates, I wasn't sure what to feel. The program started, and I listened intently to the speakers. Then Mr. Pitts took the stage. His remarks weren't extended, but they were direct. He spoke about the struggles of graduating, about how some of us had to fight tooth and nail to be there.

"Some of you knew that this day would come. I called them the children of privilege. Your parents went to college; your grandparents went to college. Growing up, you knew that this time would take place. Then there are the children of the struggle. Children like my friend, Alphonso Mayo. You are the first in your family to graduate college. You've been told that you're not good enough, that it's just not your time, that you're not worthy. You've struggled to make tuition payments. For whom, if it weren't for the impossible moments, you wouldn't be here today. Here's your opportunity to change the world. Go to someone in your community and tell them if I did it, so can you."

My mind reached back to:

- My first year in high school and being placed in 9-T.

- Contemplating the idea of dropping out.

- The 1st and 2nd-grade children I learned who to read from.

- My cousin Marcus and his influence on me.

- Mr. Cohen teaching me the significance of studying.

- My coaches, Woodson and Carter, who guided me through my athletic journey.

- The moment I departed from North Carolina Central University.

- All the events that unfolded in between.

- Most importantly, the moment I made a promise to my grandmother.

Surprisingly, they called my name to receive the Dorothy Stang Award. The award honors integrity, courage in the face of adversity, and a willingness to act on convictions without regard to consequence. They give it to the student who embodies the most cherished Stevenson values. The recipient reaches out to community members with financial, spiritual, social, or cultural needs." I don't know how I won or who voted for me, but I was grateful.

Then it was time to walk. I listen to name after name. Then, as if in a blink of an eye, it is my turn to walk across the stage and receive my degree. As I heard my name called, my heart swells with emotion. I walked up to the stage, knowing this moment was not just about me but about every moment I didn't feel wanted and abandoned. The moments when I wanted to give up or felt hopeless. The moments when I failed and was broken. It was for all those who said I couldn't do something and those who believed in me and supported me. It was for the police officer that said, ***"Look, go to school, get out of this, save yourself."***

The moment was powerful, fueled by a deep desire to break free from the generational cycles that had plagued my family for so long. I wanted to be the one to show my cousins that there was a different way, a better way. It was about living up to my true potential, something that so many of my family members had never been able to do. It was also about something more. It was a sense of loss and grief for all of the friends that I had lost to the streets, to crime, and jail. Most importantly, It was to keep my promise to my grandmother.

Speaker: *"Alphonso Mayo"*

As I walked across the stage, I looked at the sea of faces in the audience; I knew two hands were reaching out for that degree.

"We did it Ma."

The bitter-sweetness of the moment was almost too much to bear. I graduated with my Bachelor of Science in Human Service-Administration, focusing on Programs for Children. All I wanted was for my loved ones to be with me, to celebrate the milestone I had worked so hard for, and to see my grandmother smile. As the ceremony drew to a close, I lost count of the number of goodbyes I exchanged. It seemed as though every professor, student, or executive I had ever met was bidding me farewell. The atmosphere was charged with love, joy, and gratitude. I had finally accomplished something that truly mattered, and I knew I had made my children proud.

They now had a new standard of living and realized endless possibilities. I knew that this was the beginning of my journey, but I am ready to take on whatever comes my way, remembering the promise as a moment that changed my life forever. Later that evening, I checked my phone to find the final grade for my courses, a perfect 4.0. I had fulfilled my promise to my grandmother and kept my word to Ms. Parker.

"All good things must come to an end?" -Geoffrey Chaucer-

Gratitude Reflection:

Stevenson University: My Last Chance U Experience

Thank you for what you poured into me during my time at Stevenson University. I could not have been successful without the help of this unique group of people. My words can never fully express my gratitude.

- Ms. Candace Parker, who worked in admissions, for taking a chance on me and allowing me to fulfill my Promise to my grandmother.

- Tracey Cantabene, Office of Career Service, inspired me to be authentic and create my desired career.

- Mr. Rick Mason, Supervisor at PMM Cleaning Company, for believing in me by allowing me to work on campus. This allowed me to support my family. You were the father I needed, and I thank you.

- Coach Borell and Coach Thomas, for seeing my value and speaking life into me. Thank you for embracing my leadership style and loving me. Thank you for pushing me to be a better player and leader.

- Mr. Tim Campbell, the Chief Financial Officer at Stevenson University, played a crucial role, believing in me solely for my character and nothing else. During my junior year, I received a bill for over $10,000, and there was no way I could afford it. Understanding my predicament, the university dismissed the bill, instilling in me the hope I needed to honor my Promise to my grandmother. His support was pivotal in overcoming this financial hurdle.

- Ms. Christine Flax, Director of the Academic Link and the

PASS Program. Without her, I'm not sure how I would have been able to complete my career at Stevenson. I walked into the academic center looking for a tutor and left with a mentor. I left the academic center knowing I had someone who believed in me, would challenge me, and would push me to do more than I ever thought I could academically do.

- Ms. Gigi Frano, the Human Service Chair, who significantly shaped my personal and professional growth. Ms. Frano, your belief in my abilities and invaluable guidance have profoundly impacted my life. For that, I am genuinely grateful. I am incredibly grateful for your generous contributions to Mentoring Mentors. You were the first person to offer financial support, and your continued contributions each year since have been nothing short of remarkable.

- Morgan Somerville, Director of Student Engagement, for her immeasurable impact on my life. Morgan, you have been a guiding light and constant support, and I am forever indebted to you. When you gave me the book "The Other Wes Moore," little did I know that it would become a symbol of hope and inspiration for me. Through its pages, I found solace, understanding, and the belief that I, too, could overcome any obstacles that came my way. Your thoughtful gesture reminded me that you saw something in me, even when I struggled to see it myself. Your belief in my potential fueled my determination to succeed. I will never forget the moments your spirit carried me through the challenges of college. Your genuine care and concern for my well-being touched my heart in ways I can't fully express. Your support gave me the strength and confidence to persevere, even when it felt like the world was against me. What truly sets you apart, Morgan, is your ability to see the best in others and elevate them with your words and actions. You never hesitated to introduce me to others as if I were the next CEO of a Fortune 500 company or a famous person. Your belief in my potential gave me the courage to dream bigger and reach higher than I ever thought possible. Furthermore, I am grateful for your talent in connecting the dots and introducing me to other incredible individuals who share my passion and could help elevate my purpose.

- Shaniqua Parrish, my friend, reflecting on my time at Stevenson University, I am grateful for the incredible people and relationships I was fortunate to cultivate. Among them all, there's something uniquely special about our friendship that made my experience truly extraordinary. My time at Stevenson wouldn't have been the same without you. Your presence added a layer of warmth and authenticity that defined the essence of my college journey. I want to express my deepest thanks for allowing me to be my raw, unfiltered, and broken self in our friendship. Your openness and vulnerability were a source of inspiration, and I appreciate your trust in me by sharing some of your deepest pains. Watching you overcome and advocate for yourself encouraged me to be my strongest self. I am forever grateful for your impact on my life, and I want you to know that you'll always hold a special place in my heart. Thank you for being a true friend, our genuine connection, and making my time at Stevenson University unforgettable.

- Emmanuel Paul, as I reflect on our time together at Stevenson, I am filled with gratitude for the memories we shared as teammates, brothers, and great friends. Among all the teammates I had, there wasn't a single one I was prouder to play alongside than you. Even though our time together was shorter than we ever imagined, I want you to know that our friendship is something I will forever cherish in my heart. The laughter we shared, the hard work we put in together, and your constant encouragement to stay in shape are moments I will always treasure. I am grateful for how you embraced me, especially during the tough times when I struggled emotionally. You had a way of reminding me to keep pushing forward, no matter what. It saddens me deeply that you are not able to physically hold this book in your hands. But I find comfort knowing you are with us in spirit. I pray that everything I have accomplished thus far has made you proud. I will continue to honor your memory by giving my best in everything I do.

EPILOGUE

Reflecting on my life, I am reminded of the importance of pursuing one's dreams. Growing up, I faced many challenges and obstacles that made it seem impossible to achieve my goals. But even in the darkest moments, I held on to the belief that something more extraordinary and better was in store for me.

Growing up, I felt nobody cared in my home. People always gave up on me, threw me away, or counted me out. However, during my sophomore year of high school, I discovered that people listened to me. Perhaps it was the pain in my voice, a result of my troubled childhood, or my passion for living and not letting my circumstances determine my fate. My friends looked up to me, and I felt responsible for leading by example.

Although I graduated with a degree, life is life. I never expected it to be easy. Remember, I'm from Baltimore, where drugs, poverty, and hopelessness make mothers abandon their children—a place where men don't raise their sons. And where the teenage boys murder one another. Degrees can't save you here and in areas similar.

So, I searched for opportunities to make a difference in Baltimore but found little luck. After graduation, I worked two full-time jobs and volunteered as a coach and mentor. I realized that I didn't need a degree for the work I was called to do. Thinking about what to do with my life, I knew that working in childcare and with youth was my calling.

I knew the early years of our lives were crucial, shaping our social and emotional stability and laying the foundation for our future success. While I did not know much about love or affection growing up, I understood what it felt like not to have those things. Creating an environment where children felt loved, nurtured, and cared for meant everything to me, and I knew I could make a difference and help young people from going through what I had experienced. Or at least try.

In 2014, I founded a non-profit organization called Mentoring Mentors Inc. in Baltimore, MD. The organization supports youth between the ages of 11-18, helping youth develop positive relationships and positive peer influence. The social impact we are addressing is the educational and academic disparities that disproportionately affect African-American youth, particularly in urban communities. Some root causes of educational inequities are:

- Underfunded schools and programs

- Lack of resources

- Exposure to adverse environmental factors

Over the past decade, we've discovered a crucial link between social behaviors, academic outcomes, and peer relationships. We will break the cycle of disadvantages perpetuated by these disparities. Our programs improve personal, social, and leadership development to help youth establish positive peer relationships to influence educational and behavioral outcomes. This is essential for youth self-esteem, future educational and employment opportunities, financial stability, social peer groups, and overall well-being.

Through our program, we improve and increase graduation rates, increase access to higher education, increase internships and apprenticeship opportunities, and enhance our youth perspective on success.

We created the "Intergenerational Near-to-Peer Model." Our mission has evolved but has always been in alignment with redirecting youth's trajectory through college and career exposure. Our greatest strength lies in building family-like relationships with our youth. Through our work, we have seen firsthand how important it is for young people to have a sense of belonging, support, and guidance to improve their personal development, leadership skills and accountability. We have also seen how transformative it can be when given the tools and resources they need to go beyond their full potential.

Our goal is to become a residential Leadership Academy and take this model around the globe, to reach young people from every country who may feel a sense of emptiness and lack of support. We want to show them that they are not alone and that there's a community of people who believe in them and want to help them succeed. And one day, they will be the best person to help others in those same circumstances. By creating these family-like relationships, we can help young people feel safe, supported, and empowered to pursue their dreams and live beyond their full potential. This is some of the most important work we can do as a society.

As a mentor to young people, I always stress the importance of serving and making sacrifices to become a better person and create a better world. The greatest sacrifice is often the sacrifice of oneself for the benefit of others. Again, I have faced many challenges in my life, including losing my home in 2019, but I still have drive and dedication. I encourage you never to stop chasing your dreams and to continue fighting for what is in your heart and mind. Build strong connections and relationships along the way, but remember there is no true destination, only a journey.

As a Black leader seeking support in the philanthropic space, I face many challenges while seeking support. Yet, I remain committed to improving Baltimore and the world. While driving through the city, I sometimes feel that it's beyond saving and that most of it needs reinvestment. However, I know that I can impact my kids and the youth we serve. I can give them things I didn't grow up with. If I can help forty kids, I know that teaching them to serve will have a multiplier effect, sparking something that can grow and grow on its own. Because of my life, I know hope exists, even in the most unlikely places.

When you discover your true purpose, everything begins to make sense. I realized that my life had been leading me to this moment and that I had the power to make my dreams a reality. And so, with faith and determination, I embarked on a journey to pursue my passions and make a difference in the world. I want to remind you that you'll face countless setbacks and roadblocks along the way. Sometimes, you'll feel like giving up when the challenges seem too great to overcome. But, I know that if you stay true to your vision, hold on to your faith, and create a plan, you will ultimately succeed. Remember, God called you a prophet.

"We are all journeying somewhere; it's a choice between reaching our destination by design or settling for our destination by default."
-Mayo-

I want to thank you, the readers of this book. Thank you for being present. Whether you have read it, cover to cover, or just a few pages, your time and attention mean the world to me. I pray this book has inspired you to break free from the cycles holding you back and strive for a better future. Remember that you can achieve great things and that anything is possible with hard work, persistence, consistency, and a little faith.

Lastly, I would like to thank my mentor, Dr. Curry, and my Fiancé, Alexandra Porte. They both have been instrumental in my journey towards completing this book. Dr. Curry's support and mentorship has been foundational. His confidence in me and vision for me has been refreshing. His encouragement and wisdom have been a guiding light that kept me moving forward, even when the road ahead seemed uncertain.

Likewise, Alexandra has been a constant source of inspiration and strength. She has been there for me through every step of this process, offering her support, encouragement, and editing when I needed it the most. She has been here to support me through the emotional ups and downs during this process.

I am genuinely grateful for the support and love that Dr. Curry and

Alexandra have shown me throughout this journey. Their contributions to this book and my life cannot be overstated.

So, as I close this chapter of my life, I do so with gratitude and a spirit full of hope. I know there are challenges ahead, but I also know I'm not alone. With the support of the people who have been with me on this journey and with the support of all of you, I am confident that I can face whatever comes my way. Thank you for being a part of this journey, and I wish you all the best as you continue on your path, in Jesus name.

"Ma, we did it."

"In life, we must leave things behind that we care about to grow. It may seem strange that growth comes with loss, but all losses are worth God's victories for you."

-Mayo-

"Do everything as if it were the last thing you were doing in your life."
— Marcus Aurelius.

"You can't wait until life isn't hard anymore before you decide to be happy."

-Nightbird: Jane Marczewski-

Unlocking Your Potential:
Mind To Pen

Lesson 1: Redefine Your Environment

Your environment is not a determinate factor of your ultimate outcome. Your mind is.

- Write down your current environment:

- Write down an environment which you believe you could thrive:

Whatever you have written is a blueprint of what's possible. Holding this vision in your mind is the first step to bringing it into reality. Every element in your environment either uplifts and builds you for the future or erodes your potential. Understanding that what you believe is possible is crucial in shaping your future. You now have the beginning of your plan for a better future.

Lesson 2: The 15-Minute Investment

Do you have 15 minutes a day? Dedicating at least 15 minutes daily to learning, studying, or practicing with great focus can bridge any gap in your life. Can you give 15 minutes a day for 365 days?

- Write down what skills you desire.

- Write down what you want people to say about you when you die.

Building the skills needed for your desired future requires consistent, wholehearted effort. Set clear achievable goals for the next five years and keep it simple. Pick one book to read for 15 minutes daily, apply its lessons, or watch informative videos on YouTube or IG and apply the lessons.

"Knowledge is not power; applied knowledge is power."-Mayo-

Lesson 3: Discovering Your Why

- Write down your reason for wanting a better life than the one you have.

- Write down your current beliefs about why you are where you are.

- Write down where you believe you will be in 10 years. (Make it simple)

- Write down your emotions after completing the first three questions.

If your emotions don't move you to get up and want to get out of your current situation, you'll never move. Your emotions, if aligned with the proper plan, can be a driving force towards your why. Whatever you feel is what you believe and whatever you believe will determine what you're willing to do.

Lesson 4: Losing People but Adding Value

Personal growth often means letting go of certain relationships.

- Write down the individuals you are willing to part ways with to become the best version of yourselves.

- Write down why you are willing to let go.

Relationships, whether family, romantic, or friendships, should add value, not subtract value. Yes, you can learn from relationships that subtract, but you should learn more about yourself. Loyalty to oneself is paramount, and you are responsible for teaching others how to value, love, and respect you. Don't allow anyone (including your old habits and mindset) to hold you back.

Lesson 5: Your Promise to Yourself

Tip 6: Keep Promises to Yourself

- Write down or journal your promises to yourself.

- Write why you made that promise.

- Write what that promise means to you.

Develop the habit of not breaking promises to yourself. If you can do it for others, you can do it for yourself. It's the little white lies that we tell ourselves. I'm going to go on a diet but find little ways to divert from being completely disciplined. I could go on, but I think you catch my drift. Your promise should help you build self-trust and commitment.

#NeverGetComfortable

About The Authors

Alphonso Mayo, Founder and Servant leader/CEO Mentoring Mentors Inc. "Mayo," as he is affectionately known, started his career in Early childhood education after graduating from Northwestern High School in Baltimore in 2006 with his 90-hour Early Childhood Education Certification. He began his professional career in youth development in 2008. With over a decade in youth development and nearly a decade in Public Speaking, he has over 5000 speaking hours. He is closing in on 300 Social, emotional, and leadership sessions in youth development. In 2013, Alphonso was named in Who's Who Among Students in American Universities & Colleges and inducted into Tau Upsilon Alpha, the National Organization of Human Services Honor Society. Mayo is a first-generation student, graduating from Stevenson University with his Bachelor of Science in Counseling and Human Services (14), fulfilling his promise to his grandmother. In 2014, Alphonso received the Dorothy Stang Award from Stevenson University. Later, he graduated from John Hopkins University with his certification in Nonprofit Management(18) and was named Baltimore Homecoming Hero. In 2019 became a Baltimore Open Society Fellowship Recipient. In 2022, Mayo received the Young Alumni Award from Stevenson University.

Brian Nelson is a former Fulbright Scholar and the author of *The Silence and the Scorpion: The Coup Against Chávez and the Making of Modern Venezuela*. His work has been published in *The Virginia Quarterly Review, The Christian Science Monitor, and The Southern Humanities Review*, among others. He is also an adjunct professor of English at Stevenson University and an instructor for Johns Hopkins University's Center for Talented Youth. Nelson has been interviewed on TV and radio by over 50 stations throughout the United States and Latin America, including the BBC, and his work was written about in The New York Times, Foreign Policy, and Reason.

Got an idea for a book? Contact Curry Brothers Publishing, LLC. We are not satisfied until your publishing dreams come true. We specialize in all genres of books, especially religion, leadership, family history, poetry, and children's literature. There is an African Proverb that confirms, "When an elder dies, a library closes." Be careful who tells your family history. Ensure their values are your family's values? Our staff will navigate you through the entire publishing process and we take pride in going the extra mile in meeting your publishing goals.

Improving the world one book at a time!

Curry Brothers Publishing, LLC
PO Box 247 Haymarket, VA 20168
Office: (888) 726-1828

Visit us at www.currybrotherspulishing.com

www.ingramcontent.com/pod-product-compliance
Lightning Source LLC
Chambersburg PA
CBHW051145120626
46547CB00012B/954